RUMI
Soul Fury

RUMI

Soul Fury

RUMI AND SHAMS TABRIZ ON FRIENDSHIP

Translations by
COLEMAN BARKS

HarperOne
An Imprint of HarperCollins*Publishers*

HarperOne

These Rumi versions are reworked from the translations and scholarship of Ibrahim Gamard and Rawan Farhadi in *The Quatrains of Rumi*.

The Shams material is reworked from William Chittick's *Me and Rumi: The Autobiography of Shams-i Tabrizi* and Franklin D. Lewis' *Rumi, Past and Present, East and West: The Life, Teaching, and Poetry of Jalal al-Din Rumi*.

RUMI: SOUL FURY: *Rumi and Shams Tabriz on Friendship*. Copyright © 2014 by Coleman Barks. All rights reserved. Printed in the United States of America. No part of this book may be used or reproduced in any manner whatsoever without written permission except in the case of brief quotations embodied in critical articles and reviews. For information address HarperCollins Publishers, 195 Broadway, New York, NY 10007.

HarperCollins books may be purchased for educational, business, or sales promotional use. For information please e-mail the Special Markets Department at SPsales@harpercollins.com.

HarperCollins website: http://www.harpercollins.com
HarperCollins®, ✚®, and HarperOne™ are trademarks of HarperCollins Publishers.

FIRST EDITION

Designed by Ralph Fowler

Library of Congress Cataloging-in-Publication Data

Jalal al-Din Rumi, Maulana, 1207–1273.
   [Ruba'iyat. Selections. English]
   Soul fury : Rumi and Shams Tabriz on friendship / translations by Coleman Barks. — First edition.
      pages   cm
   Includes bibliographical references and index.
   ISBN 978–0–06–235098–5
   1. Friendship in literature.   2. Jalal al-Din Rumi, Maulana, 1207–1273—Translations into English.   3. Shams-i Tabrizi, –1247—Translations into English.   I. Barks, Coleman, translator.   II. Shams-i Tabrizi, –1247. Works. Selections. English.   III. Title.
PK6481.R8E54   2014
891'.5511—dc23   2014018172

14 15 16 17 18   RRD(H)   10 9 8 7 6 5 4 3 2 1

for the mystery and the glory
of friendship

Contents

Rumi

THIS DAY I CANNOT SAY—QUATRAINS

Soul Fury

EXCERPTS FROM *THE SAYINGS OF SHAMS TABRIZ*

Rumi

This Day I Cannot Say—Quatrains

Introduction: Rumi

 TANDEM CREATION

What are the qualities of a deepening awareness? To some it feels right to call that *the friend*. For others, it is more like a spaciousness, an emptiness, or silence. Many of Rumi's short poems circle around the delight, and the impossibility, of saying this blessed inwardness, the friendship. What is it to drop the ego? To let go, to surrender, to trust? All the quatrains of Rumi and all the sayings of Shams are trying, in their different and combining forms of soul fury and kindness, to help that happen in each reader. It often does not happen all at once, the final push of the ego over into the dissolution, or rebirth.

It has many names, that process of transformation. Rumi says, "I have longevity, inside this dying I have so long desired" (#3).

Rumi always works in tandem, with a friend, or friends. Or, to say it another way, his poetry is communal, with very personal touches. It is difficult to describe the process, though we all have probably experienced it. Out of his deep friendship with Shams Tabriz came the overflowing creativity of the collection he calls *The Works of Shams Tabriz,* or the *Divani Shamsi Tabriz,* often now called just *The Shams.* At the end of the poem, where the poet traditionally signs the poem by mentioning his own name, you will never find Rumi's name. Most often he mentions Shams, but sometimes another friend, Saladin Zarkub the goldsmith. Sometimes he gives the poem back into silence, sometimes into sunlight. And out of his friendship with Husam Chelebi—his scribe and chief disciple, and his tandem-work friend after Shams and Saladin were gone—came the ocean of the six books of the *Masnavi.* He calls the whole thing "The Book of Husam." Here is how the prelude to Book IV begins:

> Husamuddin! Ziya-Haqq, God's light, you draw this
> *Masnavi* out
> into the open again, your rope around its neck
> leading God knows where!

Some have expressed gratitude for this poem; this
  poem itself
lifts hands in thanksgiving, glad as a vineyard in
  summer heat.
The caravan loads up and breaks camp. Patience
  leads the way
into joy. Face down, flat on the earth.

Husam, the sun-sword of one light, many wander in
  moonlight,
but when the sun comes up, the markets open.
Exchange gets clear. Buyers and sellers can tell false
  coins from true.
Thieves recede from the scene. Only counterfeiters
and those who need to hide avoid sunlight.

Let Book IV be part of the light!

That is what his tandem creativity sounds like in action
with Husam Chelebi. It is clear evidence of Rumi's kindness.
The *interior* of a Rumi poem is friendship with a specific
human being *and* with the mystery of Allah, which he calls *the
friend,* or the unsayable absence, or daylight, or night, or the
presence inside the growing springtime green, or many other

things. Rumi's poetry is very consciously engaged in *collaborative* listening and making, the friendships and the powerful conversational dynamic going on in and around it there in the moment of its making. The poems come out of his love, and perhaps we love them for the glimpses they give of that, as well as for the light and the grief—for the taste of how it is to be, and how it is to be nothing at all.

I am not interested in placing these poems in a particular religious tradition. Rumi was a devout Muslim, a Sufi. Many of these poems are glosses on passages from the Qur'an. But he has also been heard as a more universal voice. This is what I try to bring forward. His poetry is honored and delighted in by many traditions and cultures. A great percentage of the world's people now are drawn to a sense of the sacred that is beyond belief and beyond a specific sacred text, beyond a church and a priesthood and beyond the bureaucracy of religious culture. This new and very ancient way is experiential, exploratory, and so has attracted the Sufis with their all-inclusive way of the heart.

RUMI AND KINDNESS

I met a beautiful man once, Jelaluddin Chelebi, who was at the time the head of the Mevlevi Order, the one begun by

Rumi's son. Chelebi was visiting Atlanta. He sat me down and said, "Now, what religion are you?" I raised my arms in the "who knows" gesture. "Good," he said. "Love is the religion, and the universe is the book." At the time he was the direct living descendant in the line of Rumi. "Yes!" I said quickly.

Religious traditions have served us well in some ways and ill in others. Surely it is felt as arrogance now to claim that one set of doctrines, one sacred text, is more true than another. And it is a cruel distortion of soul-compassion to *kill* people who disagree with our assertion of some *exclusive* truth. This has got to stop—the sectarian conflict, the empire and hegemony aggressions.

Of course, we must also admit that some people *do* live in a consciousness that is more compassionate and wiser than others. I once asked such a teacher, Bawa Muhaiyaddeen, what it was like to be him, as opposed to being *me*. He answered with a fable. There was once an ocean frog who came to visit a frog living in a ditch three feet by four feet and two feet deep. The frog jumped proudly all around his ditch, side to side and down to the bottom. When he came up, he asked the ocean frog, "Is this not a wonderful place to live? I am having such a fine time in this ditch."

"Yes, it *is* an amazing place," said the ocean frog.

"How is it where you live?" asked the ditch frog.

"That's hard to talk about, because where I live has no boundaries. It is infinite. It has no shore."

Bawa explained that where I lived was bounded by mind and desire. Where he lived was beyond those constrictions.

The ocean frog then says, "I may not be able to tell you about it, but someday I hope to take you there. You can be in that shoreless ocean with me."

Twenty-five years later, I came across this Taoist text by Chuang Tzu from the fourth century BCE: "The god of the North Sea said, 'You cannot discuss the *ocean* with a frog in a well—he is trapped in a confined space. You can't speak of ice to a summer insect—it is bound by one season. You can't speak of the Way with a biased scholar—he is limited by partiality. Now that you [the river god] have come out through the cliffs and gazed at the great sea, you know your relative insignificance; now it is possible to talk to you of the great underlying pattern.'"*

Bawa had used the old Taoist story to answer my question. (The parable probably has many lineages.) He was open to truth from any culture and from every human life. When you came into his room, he always wanted to know what you had

* Adapted from Michael D. Coogan, ed., *Eastern Religions* (London: Duncan Baird Publishers, 2005), 248.

been doing earlier that day. Then he would use that as a point of reference. The great teachers and saints of every tradition know that there is a table where we can all sit down, everybody in this mysterious, hilarious family.

So I agree with those two Jelaluddins, Chelebi and Rumi. Love, together with kindness, *is* the religion that we must learn to practice more and more deeply, in all the many ways that there are to love. This universe and our lives as we are daily leading them *are* the book that we delight in studying, this shared experience of being alive. The excitement and the depth of sharing—that friendship—are some of what Rumi and Shams are teaching. May we read this superbly edited text (the world) long and well together. The mountains, the animals, the breathing plants and wildflowers, the languages and dialects, what happens in the news each day, the mineral deposits, the billions of galaxies, the four hundred billion stars with their solar systems in just our Milky Way, this new grandson Henry running down the hall "doing laps." Lord.

RUMI'S LIFE

Jelaluddin Rumi was born near the city of Balkh, in Vahksh, in what is now Afghanistan, then on the eastern edge of the

Persian Empire, on September 30, 1207. He descended from a long line of Islamic jurists, theologians, and mystics. When Rumi was still a young man, his family left Balkh ahead of the invading Mongol armies under Genghis Khan, who was extending his empire westward, eventually all the way to the Adriatic. It is said that Rumi's father, Bahauddin, loaded ninety camels with just books for the journey. Theirs was a profoundly learned lineage.

Rumi and his family went to Nishapur and then on to Damascus, where the poet and teacher Fariduddin Attar recognized the teenage boy as a great spirit. He is reported to have said, as he saw Bahauddin walking toward him with Rumi a little behind, "Here comes a sea, followed by an ocean." To honor this insight, he gave Rumi a copy of his own *Ilahinama* (*The Book of God*).

The family eventually settled in Konya, now in south-central Turkey, where Bahauddin resumed his role as head of the *medrese,* the dervish learning community. Rumi was still in his twenties when his father died several years later, and he became head of the *medrese*. He gained a wide reputation as a devout scholar, and his school reportedly numbered over ten thousand students. The work of Rumi's community was to open the individual and collective heart. They used music and poetry and movement. They sat in silence. They listened to discourses. Stories, jokes, meditation—everything was used. They fasted and they feasted. The cook, Ahim Baaz, was an important figure in Rumi's community. You can visit his tomb in Konya today. The members walked together. They worked in the garden and the orchard. They observed animal behavior very closely. It was a kind of scripture that they read for signs.

This was not a renunciate group. Everyone had a family and a line of useful work. They were masons, grocers, weavers, hatmakers, carpenters, tailors, bookbinders. Everyone was deeply engaged. They were affirmative, ecstatic makers. Some call them Sufis. I like to say they were living the way of the heart.

A few years after Bahauddin's death in 1231, Burhan Mahaqqiq, a hermit meditator in the remote mountain region north and east of Konya, returned to learn that his teacher, Rumi's father, had died. He decided to devote the rest of his life to training his teacher's son. For nine years he led Rumi on many forty-day fasts (*chillas*), sometimes as many as three in a row. Rumi became a joyful adept in this mystical tradition.

Rumi's son, Sultan Velad, saved 147 of his father's personal letters, so, amazingly, we have an accurate sense of what his daily life was like eight centuries ago. He was deeply involved in the details of community life. In one letter, he begs a man to put off, for fifteen days, collecting the money he is owed by another man. In another he asks a wealthy nobleman to help a student with a small loan. Someone's relatives have moved into the house of a devout old woman; he tries to solve the situation. Sudden lines of poetry are scattered throughout the practical business contained in the letters. His life is grounded simultaneously in the daily necessities *and* in ecstatic creativity. His kindness is everywhere apparent in these letters. He is so practical and attentive to what needs to happen, what could make a situation more fluid, more *kind* for those involved. He is always trying to remove whatever blocks the flow of love, money for loans, education, the ease of friendship within a community, a household, a family.

It was probably in the late fall of 1244 that Rumi met Shams Tabriz, a fierce man-God, God-man. Shams had wandered through the Near East in search of a soul friend on his level. He never stayed anywhere long. Whenever students began to gather around him, as they inevitably did, he excused himself for a drink of water, wrapped his black cloak around him, and was gone. The facts about Shams' life are just as elusive as he was. He *may* have been born in 1185. He *may* have died in 1248. He *may* be buried in Konya, but it seems most likely now that it was in Khuy, Iran, near Tabriz. He was known as *Parinda,* "Flier" (or "Bird"). In his restless searching, he asked that God's hidden favorite be revealed to him, so that he could learn more about the mysteries of divine love. An inner voice came: *What will you give in return?*

"My head," said Shams.

The one you seek is Jelaluddin of Konya, son of Bahauddin of Balkh.

When Shams arrived in Konya, he took lodging at the caravanserai of the sugar merchants, pretending to be a successful seller of sugar. But all he had in his room was a broken water pot, a ragged mat, and a headrest of unbaked clay. One day, as Shams sat at the gate, Rumi came riding by on a donkey, surrounded by students. Shams rose and took the bridle.

"Money changer of the current coins of esoteric significance, knower of the names of the Lord, tell me who is greater, Muhammad or Bestami?"

"Muhammad is incomparable among the saints and prophets."

"Then how is it he said, 'We have not known You as You should be known,' while Bestami cried out, 'How great is my glory!'?"

Rumi heard the depth of the question and fell to the ground in astonishment. When he revived, he answered, "For Muhammad, the mystery was always unfolding, while Bestami takes one gulp and is satisfied."

The two tottered off together. They spent weeks and months at a time together in the mystical conversation known as *sohbet*.

Another version of their meeting goes this way: One day Rumi is teaching by a fountain in a small square in Konya. Books are open on the fountain's edge. Shams walks quickly through the students and pushes the books into the water.

"Who are you, and what are you doing?" Rumi asks.

"You must now live what you have been reading about."

Rumi turns to the books in the fountain, one of them his father's beloved spiritual diary, the *Maarif.*

Shams says, "We can retrieve them. They will be as dry as they ever were." He lifts out the *Maarif* to show him. "Dry."

Shams seems to have successfully weaned Rumi from any dependence on his father Bahauddin's book. But one night Rumi dreams he is reading that book again. When he wakes, Shams walks into Rumi's room and scolds him for going back to his old ways. Rumi says that he has not looked at that book for a long while. Shams laughs and begins relating Rumi's entire dream. "Dreams express our waking thoughts." So long as Shams was alive, Rumi did not touch that book again.

As Rumi began his relinquishment of books and borrowed awareness, the real poetry began to come. "What I had thought of before as God, I met today in a human being." The meeting with Shams is the central event in Rumi's life. They were together in Konya for about three and a half years. Twice during that time Shams left abruptly, perhaps to help Rumi move to the next stage of soul growth. "Separation cooks," Shams often said. Or perhaps Shams was forced out of the community by the jealousy of some of Rumi's disciples. What happened is the subject of extensive debate among the scholars. When Shams disappeared altogether, he may have been killed by those jealous disciples, among them Rumi's own son, Ala al-Din. Franklin Lewis, however, who has done the most exhaustive research on this, feels that Shams left to give Rumi the final push needed in his soul's development. In the small town of Khuy, near Tabriz, there is a tower named after Shams. Lewis thinks that Shams may be buried there or nearby.

Shams' murder is the version of the story that came down in the oral tradition among the Mevlevi dervishes. In that account, Shams came to Sultan Velad in a dream after he had been killed and told him what had happened. We can only speculate what the truth is about Shams' disappearance. Another story has come down that Rumi went out looking for Shams. One day, walking a Damascus street, he realized that he *was* their friendship. He had *embodied* it. He returned to Konya and lived out his life in that realization.

The miracle and mystery of their friendship, and of the creation generated by it—the poetry, the music, the community, the exfoliating friendships—these cannot be approached with language. We can *feel* the power and depth, the harsh strength of Shams' presence, but silence is probably the best way to approach him. As the wise elder tells Rumi,

> *Some things cannot be told*
> *or understood, only seen*
> *and lived within.*
> #11

Over the course of his life, Rumi had two wives. By the first, Gowher Khatun, he had two sons, Ala al-Din and Sultan Velad. When she died in 1242, he married Kira Khatun, by whom he had another son, Mozaffer, and a daughter, Malika. There is a wonderful hagiographic story about Kira Khatun. One day she peered through a slit in the door into the room where Rumi and Shams were sitting in *sohbet*. She saw one of the walls open and six majestic beings enter. They bowed and laid flowers at Rumi's feet, although it was the middle of winter. They remained until time for dawn prayers, which they motioned for Shams to lead. He excused himself, and Rumi performed the duties. Then the six left, and when Rumi came out from the chamber, he saw his wife in the hall. He gave her the flowers, saying, "Some visitors brought these for you."

The next day she sent her servant to the perfumer's market with a few leaves and blossoms from the bouquet. They were unable to identify the flowers, until a spice trader from India recognized them as flowers that grow only in Sri Lanka. The servant went back with this astonishing news, and while she was telling Kira, Rumi came in and told her to take good care of the flowers, because some Indian saints had brought them from the paradise that human beings had lost. As long as Kira Khatun lived (she died nineteen years after Rumi), the flowers stayed fresh and fragrant, and just a single leaf applied to a diseased eye or other injured part brought instantaneous healing.

Many stories have come down to us about Rumi. Some have to do with animals. He was in tune with the animal mind, much like an indigenous shaman. The same attunement to others that brings out his kindness in the letters gives him closeness with animals. Here is a story that I love. Some butchers purchased a heifer, and they were leading her to be slaughtered. Suddenly she broke free and ran. They shouted after her, which made her more crazed. No one could get near her. Rumi was walking the same road, with his disciples some distance behind. When the heifer saw him, she trotted over and stood very still beside him as though communing with him. He rubbed and patted her neck. When the butchers came to claim their property, he pleaded for her life. His students joined in the discussion. Rumi used the situation. "If a simple animal, being led to its death, can take such lovely refuge with me, how much more beautiful must it be when a human being puts heart and soul in the care of God?" The entire group, dervishes and butchers alike, found such joy in these words that they began to play music. Dancing and spontaneous poetry continued into the night.

Another animal story features dogs. Rumi was giving a longer than usual discourse in the square. People wandered away. The sun was going down. All that was left was a line of seven dogs, sitting on their haunches, listening attentively. "These are my true students," he said. At the end of his life, he had a cat that he loved. When he died, she died soon after. It is said that his daughter, Malika, insisted that he be buried with the cat lying on his chest, the way they loved to do.

For the last twelve years of his life, Rumi wrote, or dictated, one long, luminous walkabout poem, the *Masnavi,* which is sixty-four thousand lines of poetry divided into six books. It is one of the great treasures of world literature. As he walked around Konya with his scribe, Husam Chelebi, Rumi spoke this poem as part of his teaching and the continuous attention he gave to his community and the soul-growth needs of specific individuals.

Rumi died at sunset on December 17, 1273. Thousands still visit his tomb in Konya each month. One of the inscriptions there is, "Do not look for him here, but rather in the hearts of those who love him." It is said that representatives of all religions came to his funeral. When asked why they came, each said that Rumi and his poetry had deepened them in their own faith.

In my renderings of Rumi, I try to explore this universalist aspect. He is our great planetary poet. It doesn't seem right to stress how divided and in conflict we are, with the many (four hundred or so) religions and their sometimes mutually exclusive, competing truths. Rumi brings a healing peacefulness. Legend has it that when the Mongol armies under Bughra Khan got close to Konya, Rumi walked out alone to speak with the general. The authority of Rumi's presence was such that the general decided not to sack Konya. "There may be others like this man there," he said. So, however naïve it may be, in this violent world, I would rather see us as walking along inside the mystery of friendship, with its soul fury and its kindness, to sit down together finally at the table that Rumi, and many others, have set.

This Day I Cannot Say

1.

As long as I am alive, this,
this is who I am and what I do.

My peace, my resting place, what I want
and its satisfaction, truth.

By *this,* I mean this day
I cannot say, this love.

This being that is after me,
that I am after, quarry
chasing quarry.

2.

Find your place and close your eyes,
so your heart can start to see.

When you give up being self-absorbed,
your being becomes a great community.

3.

I am grumpy about one thing:
I feel such peacefulness.

Ill-tempered, within this ease
of being. I am a royal falcon
in the shape of an owl.

I have longevity, inside this
dying I have so long desired.

4.

Out of kindness comes this world,
and certain arrangements of stars.
With just the right conjunction, you appear.

One drop of your kindness
makes the ocean sweet.

One grain from that granary
makes an empty acre open myriad,
like a cornfield in the sun.

5.

Every day at dawn you set your tent up by the stream.
You move patterns of fragrance in the garden wind.

This friendship we share is a tambourine,
where, on the circle of its face, in sacred concert,
you make, every moment, a thousand touches.

6.

Love, what sort of thing are you?
You carry so much along.

You gather many together,
and then scatter them. You love to stay home
and let everything else keep watch at your door.

Love, you are the mother,
every human being is your child.

7.

I wander through the towns of this world,
leaving them each to those in charge
of decorating them for festivals.

Like a boat drifting on the ocean
with no set direction, one afternoon
resting in a caravanserai, that night,
starting out for somewhere else.

 8.

Tonight we are here
with a thousand hidden mystics,
concealed, and absolutely obvious,
like the soul, *self-evident.*

Musicians, soul-knowers,
everybody, keep looking.

We need to find more
of these invisible dancers.

9.

My thirsty heart, swift-running stream,
not randomly falling along,
but strong and sure, you are not one
who keeps quiet his longings
closed inside his chest.

You, the spring-source of speech,
be always talking more, more.

10.

Look how dust-grains make the sun
look like it's raining fire,
or like the world-tree in full bloom
with this awake and talking dust,
so unaware who gives it beauty,
or what is coming through
its growing intelligence.

11.

Last night, alone with a wise elder, I said,
Please. Do not hold back from telling me
any secrets about this universe.

Leaning near, he spoke into my ear,
Some things cannot be told
or understood, only seen
and lived within.

 12.

I walk the city at night, like the wind,
like rain. Can you get to sleep by doing this?
Intellect looks to place things in context.
Do not expect that from me.

13.

We have a different intention now,
with minds alive in a new way.
The beloved has a more fluid beauty
that even love does not satisfy.

Autumn will bring a sky
so vast and empty
that something entirely fresh
will begin to grow next spring.

14.

Listen to the lord of all birds,
parrot free of any cage,
child of a soul-secret, king
of language, breaker of cages.
Listen to yourself,
and break out of your cage.

15.

As long as you have not set fire
to everything you call *yours,*
you are not alive. You are not *here*!
Your happiness is not real.

A true wandering pilgrim
sleeps on bedding of flame.
Burn, as you rove the world,
or you are not walking with us.

 16.

Discover the world
that moves in us like blood,
that never stops, never sleeps.
It does not matter if wild impulses are there,
unconsciousness; it does not matter what
flows inside you, because the great shaman,
the *changer,* creation itself, also moves
in that bloodlike moving.

That motion is closer to each of us
than the big vein on our necks.

17.

With love, there is one step, then another,
the most real being the step from
pre-existence into existence.

You think that in nonexistence
you see many different beings. Not so.
Rub your eyes and look again.

In nonexistence, there is only not-ness,
annihilation-in-God, everywhere only that.

18.

Here we are in this clay and water mud.
But a grand creating does appear
out of the body, so that when I call out
for one like you, you answer inside my calling:

Here   I   am
    (I)   (am)   (here)

for one like you.

19.

As long as you do not extinguish your self,
the flame of ego will keep you from
the experience of union.

That does not come from God descending into you,
but rather from your not-being,
which does not happen with just talking about it.

 20.

A swift stream never gets bored
with the fish that swim in it.

Nor do those fish weary
of feeling the flow around them.

No. This world loves its lovers,
and those lovers never tire of being
so dear and near what bears them along.

21.

This bird is free of its cage.
This cage, released of its bird.
Both so empty, so ecstatic,
that they let fragrance come
through this song, eternity in tears.

22.

I ask the reed flute, Why are you crying?
How can there be such tears
when nothing has been lost?

The reed flute says, Not so.
They took me from the lips
that once made sugar throughout
my whole and silent body.

Now I live letting others
make crying sounds
with my emptiness.

23.

The friend says a presence builds and circles
in images that come from language,
but do not be hypnotized
by these motions.

Look for something
that circles around *me*.

 24.

Dear one, dear to me as the soul,
so unsettled and wanting to wander.
Sit down *inside* your wanderlust.

Your feet have been wounded
in the search. Maybe your final steps,
your falling-down, is *here*.

✤ 25.

Are you in rose fragrance? No.
Do the sun and stars see you? No.

You say, *It is night.*
Look there in the window.

But it can only be night
if you leave. Otherwise, no.

✤ 26.

You are the ruby, the agate, pearl, ocean,
free of location, but firmly grounded.

Master spirit, generosity,
for you coming late is fine, so come late,
with your perfect timing. Just right.

27.

Joseph, my soul, ask about
your father, Jacob.

Mercy, don't you wonder
how Job is doing in his troubles?

All the beautiful ones
are dolls you play with.

As for us, where have *we* gone?
Ask separation. He will know.

28.

Here is a subtle truth.

Beloved, lovely face from Chigil,
there is a way from heart to heart,
but I do not live within your eye.

You are the living lightpoint
in *my* eye. I am
this fragile human face.

29.

Someone who knows your face,
do they care about a rose garden?

Someone familiar with your love,
do they worry about candles and lamps?

Some say the mind's vigor grows strong
with sleep. Does a lover care about his mind?

 30.

The hearts of lovers make a great river.
A single lover is foam riding that.

Your body is a millstone.
Love, the riverwater.

How can the body turn
and do its work
with no water in the millrace?

31.

A certain one claps his hands.
That makes me clap mine.
His heart changes my heart.
He makes me undignified, unreasonable.
I used to have those qualities.

Now I have become whatever
that one wants: a child, a stern judge,
a wandering beggar, singing.

 32.

I am a mountain. What I say
is an echo of what you say.
I am a painting being painted.

I am the lock. A key slips in
to help me make an opening sound.

This talking is not mine.

33.

Someone ties a length of rope
into a complicated knot.

He is making a joke about how *he* is,
and how things go in the world.

There is a lot of discussion
about union and separation.
But how can something
that was never apart
come back together?

34.

That king for whom I am
his lunatic clown, through whose love
I have found a home,
sends me an official letter,
stamped with his seal.
It says, *I am yours.*

For that moth-surrender,
a shelf of a hundred candles
suddenly flames up.

35.

Pure scoundrels.
We just do not care
what anyone thinks.

Broken open like this
since eternity began,
we start to spill again.

We rub the dregs on our heads.
We smear dreg-darkness
blame on our faces.

36.

With love, there is no judging.
Who has more or less,
who is more wild, or more in control?

With love, there is no reciting
of scripture, no teacher-student anything,
only silly pranks,
games that mean nothing,
and lots of laughing.

37.

A love comes,
and other loves become longings
for that love. I burn to ash inside it,
to NOT-being, nothing. *Not.*

Now those ashes burn again,
alive in a thousand light-forms.

38.

There is a cave inside you.
Far back at the end of that cave
is a brightly lit market square.

Everyone has a deep friend
and something that they love to do,
a beloved and a craft.

But this lively market
in the far reaches of the cave within you
is more amazingly *hidden*
than anything you have yet found.

39.

Wind.   Leaves.
How could you not tremble
when I move through?

What can you do
but the work I ask you to?

I have thrown a stone
and broken your water jar.
You have no choice now.

You *must* become ocean, pearls—
all the living amazement found
in a hundred bodies of water.

40.

As the soul's great peace circles my heart,
you circle my shy soul.

Like a tree, I raise my head
inside your rainy wind, laughing
as your turning holds me.

41.

There is a wine for anyone thirsty for love.
Springwater too will be set before you.

We live in a ruin, this body,
where treasure is buried.
You are that treasure.

Try to wake from this dream we live.
Don't be afraid. *Wake up!*

 42.

There is a same-breath companion
who gives you the desire
to come into a sacred place.

Breathe and taste that breathing
to the end. Call it grace,
or vast generosity.
It is not some teasing *amour.*

43.

Last night I left the radish-sellers,
and went back to the dear soul-companions,
from unripe grapes to sweet grape juice.

I went from those who love the dark
out into the moon's round light.

Then I went to sleep
with those who are fully awake.

44.

The friend wants me to jump out of myself,
then to remain free in the air of the jump.

I find myself moving through
certain spirit-stations,
but each of them is still
a prison cell, a holding-back.
He wants me beyond
all stopping points.

45.

What I want is beyond
this world and the next.
The joy of my soul is such
that when you open
your mouth to laugh,
inside your laughter,
I open into that which is
beyond all openings.

 46.

You have come—you are here—you never left.
Swift-running creek that stays the same
is one of your truest names.

Musk in the air: we are the fragrance.
Have you ever known a scent
apart from the air you breathe it in?

❋ 47.

I see so clearly into my own life
how it would be good *not*
to see with these eyes.

What can I *do,*
so that I see
more with your eyes?

❋ 48.

There is that in you
that knows what is sacred
and starts moving toward it,
without your choosing to.

In your human clay,
a jewel of knowing, unknowing.

Like a polo ball controlled by the deft mallet
of the most expert rider you can imagine.

That great athlete moves
you through the field.
He has you, all his.

49.

When a dervish has truly broken open,
that condition is not something imaginary.

The place, the self, that he or she lives in then,
becomes a royal encampment better than
any location, better than existence,
better than the turning universe.

 50.

People who work are not appropriate
for this group. We move along
like roving, sometimes-bandit, rascals
and unemployable bums.

Successful, proud of your wealth?
No place for you here.

51.

Not that, no. Not that.

I cannot go back to something less.

I do not want a rabbit. No gazelles.

I love lions, but only *that* lion.

 52.

I did not know your company in the cave.

I did not feel that grace of longing.

Anything there is a lot of becomes cheap.

I have a lot of longing for you now,

but it does not, and never will, come cheap.

53.

Seeing your face makes my night day.
Breathing with you, fools become the guides
we need. Blind pilgrims find their way.

Any night now no doubt, the bald
will go to sleep and wake with hair!

 54.

I am the one who loves your face.
I stand in the doorway
of *your* house.

You say, *Quit standing here in my doorway.*   *Leave.*
My friend, if I were not standing *here,*
I would not exist.

55.

My salamander soul
feels so at home in the fire
of longing. It is like a wine
taking me into sleep and dream.

 56.

Just before dawn
there comes deadly deep sleep,
a wolf that takes both strong and weak.

Snore-khor-khor-snore,
you say back to me.

Splash nightwater on your face.
Put your hands down in the dew.
Now put them wet on your face,
your arms, your feet.
Cleanse yourself as you do
before and after prayer.

Wake for the blessing coming
then *before* sunlight returns.

57.

When you search for the home
of the soul, you become the soul.

Wanting a taste of bread,
you become the oven.

Understand this much: whatever
you love and look for, you are.

58.

Ocean-heart, gamble away all your coral,
your pearls, your platinum fish.

There is no other way for a der-fish.
Open your mouth like an oyster,

like the body saying *ahhh,*
ready for the soul to enter.

59.

They brought us here from the tavern,
arguing, of course, but not
argumentative. In that eternity-tavern
where we were, everything is tangled,
but threading through flows
something harmonious and whole,
as honey and milk become
as they are being stirred together.

 60.

I stole this whirling from my soul.
Before being in the body,
I was moving like this.

They tell me patience and being still
are better. I prefer to move.

You can have my stillness and my patience
as a gift. Please. You're welcome.

61.

You come with a message
that will make me smile,
but you hide it.

Such things cannot be hidden.
Even if you put a sign on a garden gate
that says PRISON, the garden will
still be in there, *gardening.*

62.

Every day you bring me soul-promptings
that drive me *out,* new ideas, enthusiasms.
Your generosity is an ocean of delight.

But now from the same source comes
my desire for fresh-cooked fish
and just-baked bread.

63.

I keep asking, Who gives my soul
this increasing delight in what it does?
Who gave me life in the first place?

Sometimes I feel covered
like a falcon mewed,
waiting inside its hood.

Other times, I can *see*.
Then I get released into sky.

64.

There is a life where you have
your longed-for companion
day and night, night and day.

There is a way beyond time,
a being who gives us
the purest clear to drink,
and is at once cup, wine,
water, grace, eternity.

65.

There is a kind of wildness that makes
a man, or woman, conspicuous.

He, or she, is riding a horse of great longing,
and anyone who recognizes that
is just as daft in a divine way and known to be,
by those wild others, their friend.

66.

My heart wanders along a way,
until it comes to an emptiness, a desert,
where even the way wonders, *How did we get* here?

A lover runs wildly into the mountains,
where, because of his love,
a hundred new mountains come near.

67.

Get up. Turn around the *qutb* of your time
as pilgrims wind the Kaaba on the plain of Arafat.

How did you manage to get so mired in mud?
Move. Movement will open blessings.

 68.

Your mind may be bound tight,
but your feet are free.
Move them apart, walk along,
run.   Now, dance!

This is one secret for unbinding
stuck thought: loosening bodily
constriction becomes soul-expansion.

There is the water of the well
and the water of the stream.

Consider how those two
have different qualities,
each with a beauty of its own.

69.

My soul is one. My body, a hundred thousand.
Whether you call me body or soul does not matter.
I am both one and many.

With work and love, I have made myself
into another, so that the other one,
whom I also *am,* might be pleased.

70.

My soul is one. My body,
a hundred thousand beings.

Since I am *all of that,*
I cannot speak of anything but myself.

My head rises up like a wave,
like an individual soul,
but notice how
the wave that lifts out now
falls back into the ocean.

71.

You are my Joseph. I am the grieving Jacob.
You are the body's health. I am Job, afflicted.

But how could I *be anyone,*
since you are the friend inside everyone?

I clap my hands to hear your feet
dance against the ground.

72.

A riddle: What is it
that gives form such great joy,
and without which all appearances
grow dull, drained of pleasure?

In one moment that *something* slips away.
In the next, out of nowhere,
it comes back and knocks form to pieces.

Answer: *Your face.*

73.

There is no finer friend
than the freedom of solitude.

No occupation better
than nothing-to-do.

As you give up your mind,
that trickery and cunning,
you become truly crafty.

74.

Oceans move, always in motion, because of love.
Clouds condense to rain for the same cause.

Lightning falls to the ground. Smoke
rises into nightsky, all for love.

75.

Always awake, love never sleeps,
never falls into sleeping eyes.

One subject now remains
that I will not expound upon.

I will not say anything because
you have never spoken of it.

76.

Repeat these sentences
until night comes:
Our days have no nights.
There are no rules with love.

Love is an ocean with no shore
where many are drowning,
but no one calls out for help,
Lord, Lord, as they become the sea.

✤ 77.

The Taurus bull in the nightsky
never felt like this. This is
more than all the lovers.
My soul now is your soul.

Go inside and ask, Is this what
everyone feels? It has to be.

✤ 78.

No longer under anyone's command.
Free. Say to yourself, *Lord*.

Let the arrow of looking land
wherever it finds itself, no longer
attached to ego, persona, nothing
other than a deep core of being.

A fine place to live,
where the self can beat the drum
of ecstasy and majesty.

79.

I have been running,
following my heart for so long,
exhausted, to a place where I am not,
here, with no location.

Not until I lost both self and world
could I say, and it be said of me,
Nothing. Neither this nor that.

 80.

The longing that makes you sit secluded,
that longing eventually takes
the human shirt off your back.

Strange being then,
neither seeker nor sought.

Who can be a breath-companion
with one who has no breath?

81.

Thick-growing green, you make us dance.
Orchard, tall oak, rose, you hold
the excitement we feel.

You give new trembling
to those we thought were dead,
best friend and teacher ever,
you inside the growing.

 82.

Green of the garden, every tree, solitude,
my good luck, the *rain-listening* music.

Without you, none of this intimate
and outer excitement is anything
but a sad show, depressing.
Come, stay longer.

83.

One who opens hearts has come.
Do not constrict yourself against that.
Be smoothed into generosity.

Fly wings look pitiful next to
the wingspan of the great firebird
flown here from Mount Qaf: Shams Tabriz.

84.

First, you hold me in your arms,
and all is well.

Then, you give me to those who rob us
of beauty, the death-dealers,
and all is well.

After death, you offer another kind
of life, and all is well.

85.

I have a friend who is my sun,
our sun, also the garden, the moon,
the stars, a room we go to with others
to talk, a sheltered bench on the roof
where we can be alone.

A friend who is our prayer rug,
our discipline with fasting, the feast
on the evening we honor Abraham,
the exalted feel of a Night of Power.

As inspiration comes, this friend
is each of those for all of us.

86.

Last night, like a moon, no, the sun,
no, more than my imagination
can reach around, beauty
I cannot fathom, was here.

87.

You want me more awake. You want
more tears to come with this longing.

Silently, you take me to a stream
and throw me into the grandeur
of your surrendering.

88.

I say one line. You turn away.
Are you trying to put me in that?

Would you discourage me from writing? I ask.
You say, *No house built in that way*
will ever hold me.

89.

The friend tells me, *You will not see me*
in your dreams again. Some years must pass.

Then he says to the night, *You will not see me*
until the early dawn-radiance
comes up inside you.

90.

I am a mirror, as well as someone
suddenly met. Lost in the taste of eternity,
I turn pain away; I heal the soul.

Clear, cold springwater, as well as someone
bringing you a glass of wine.

91.

When you feel drawn to this love of mine,
go outside the six directions:
north-east-south-west, above and below,
now folded down on one another.

Go *inside* the love-ocean of heart.
You are my soul friend already.
Still, you stand on the bank and look.

92.

We load world-baggage onto nonexistence
and laugh at the absurdity, the deception.

Now, bit by bit, as though playing
a knife-dance with our hands,
we cut the ropes.

The sky-tent of patience comes down,
along with everybody's equanimity.

93.

How much longer
do I have to see these colors
and smell and taste this world
so set inside time?
When will I see my intricate
and subtle soul friend again,
who, when I look at him, I see myself,
who, when I look at
myself, I see him.

 94.

I see the one I do not see.
I hear dear words from one
I cannot be with, that taste
on my lips.   *Ya-Sin.*
No one knows what those
letter combinations mean
at the beginning of certain
chapters of the Qur'an.
Ya-Sin, the unseen one
keeps me getting up from
where I'm never sitting long.

95.

There is pain in this longing,
and not so much of what we call joy.

We long for friends, but the healing
of that does not come, just the longing.

I wonder what I will say
when I see him again.

Then I meet my friend
and cannot speak.

96.

I speak to you, not making a sound,
sentences unavailable to ears.

No one's ears but yours
hear what I say, though
I am speaking to a crowd.

97.

In this book of the heart that we guard, you and I,
you have written something that we must read together.

As you say, *Only when*
we are alone together.

These words here also are about
that which will be understood only
within each other's presence.
Not until then.

98.

We were so fresh before,
when we were entirely heart and soul,
not weighed down with bodies.

If grace allows, if the lord forgives,
we shall return to how it was before.
As we began in the first creation,
we will do it again. . . .

99.

Brought here from the tavern called
Am I Not (Yes!) Your Lord?
A-lastu bi-rabbi-kum?
With *Na-am! (Yes!)*, our answer,
said simultaneously.

Disheveled, nervous, I came,
and I will be taken back
in whatever state I am in
when that finally happens.

However it was I came from nonbeing,
the crossing back over will occur,
and so it goes, nonexistence to being,
Am-I-Not (Yes!) tavern to earth-tavern,
then back to *Am-I-Not (Yes!)*.

100.

I have been around these ecstatic lovers
so long that I am weak with love,
fed up with being reasonable.

Carry me off and put me with them.

101.

These eyes that weep?
A cloud passing across.
Tears? *Water mirage.*

This heart? You say,
A piece of roasting meat.

This body? *The ruins we walk.*

102.

Gamble everything for union.
Casual stories are not enough.

Skim milk does not appeal to those
who love wine. At the long table
where those who are completely free
sit down, not one sip is given to ego.

103.

Wandering like planets wander,
like Venus walking over to Saturn
with her music, *I want my soul.*
I want the source of every soul.

Owls look for a city in ruins,
with no people. I am not an owl.

104.

I am not this body, this form
that draws lovers together. Rather,
I am a taste of something *inside* you.

That taste may occur to you suddenly
while I am talking, or when you hear my name.
Or while saying, *Allah, Allah.*

Hold on to it. Observe it carefully.
Find its value and give thanks.
That *taste* is what I am.

105.

If you find yourself, even for a moment,
as a companion of the friend,
that moment, you may feel, is the most
you will know of happiness in this life.

Do not waste such a rare instant.
You may not have another.

 106.

A perfect love, that beauty is here.
My heart fills with speech,
yet I say nothing.

Very strange. With my thirst so ready
to be slaked, and pure clean water
flowing here in front of me,
still I do not bend down to drink.

107.

Besides this, there is another way
of speaking. Besides heaven and hell,
there is somewhere else that we can go.

For those who are free, there is a way in
to another soul. The secret of that
is one that we shall keep.

 108.

I have read so many stories
about lovers and beloveds, the ache
of a heart that has been hurt
and still is breaking.

But this friendship is something different,
with less pathos. It is the entire foundation
of a capital city, a grandeur of presence,
one that can be called on as *you.*

This that we have does not appear
in the old love stories.

109.

If you were to string together a hundred long days,
with no nights in them, and sing
your longing-songs for all that time,
the soul would still not be impressed.

And if you do not understand
this surrendered-heart poetry of mine,
you are living mostly in your mind.

 110.

What do I *believe*? Your eyes. My *faith*?
The shape of your head, your face.

Some say about us, *Those two,*
what they have is not religion.

But I met the truth of *religion*
in your shattered surrendering.

111.

We are lovers of love, of pure freedom,
Khidr tasting the life-spring.

Sometimes that love-king gives a traveler
a letter of safe passage, special privileges,
and access to the treasury. But not all
are given the taste of such blessing.

 112.

This I feel has nothing to do
with silver money, or silk.
It is the same in fear as it is
when the actual troubles come.

I feel the great joy of let-go,
unlike you, my friend, with
your pretend-surrender.

113.

We have found a salve that heals,
a way to offer breath.

As every moment's in-breath
becomes the next breath-out,
love comes alive inside
our breathing.

114.

Since the moment I first loved you
and knew your soul in that way,
we have played many secret afternoon
games, backgammon, chess,
and I have lost so completely,
that now you walk gracefully, freely,
the empty pavilion that is my heart.
Nothing else is here.

115.

Nonexistence is preparing
more tasty experiences,
tray on tray coming down.

You put bites of food in your mouth;
you chew thoughtfully.

Great pleasures arrive from there
where there are no candy shops.

On the way is stage after stage
of living awareness, levels
opening on other levels.

116.

In my soul I have sad desire,
a longing. No. It is more
a shining about to leave the air,
a dust-mote goodbye. The whole
atmosphere is in love with you.

117.

Some are saturated with this world,
tired of it, but still hungry for you.

Warrior heroes fear
being separated from you.

The gazelle's wide eyes are beautiful,
but not so much next to yours.

Lions hiding in undergrowth are held
in the strength of your tall-grass hair.

118.

Friend, could anything be more pleasure
for the fig-seller than selling figs?

We live in a soul-drunk state,
ecstatic. We die like this, and always
we are running, running toward
the gathering they call our last time together.

119.

My soul and yours are essentially one.
My appearance, my inwardness,
and the way you are in the world,
the way you are invisibly,
all these are the same now.

It would be naïve to talk of differences,
what is mine, what is yours. Untrue.
Those terms no longer apply.

 120.

As floodwaters rise around your house,
the cup of your real life begins to fill.

Be happy. One blink,
and the hired man comes
who carries all you own away.

121.

From wildflowers in the field
I take in *your* fragrance.

In the color of the tulip
and the jasmine I see you.

When I am not near these,
I say your name to myself,
so I can *hear* the evidence.

 122.

If you leave this life, I will leave my life.
If you leave my heart, I shall too.

Still, in the way of things, I am a bow.
Bending to pray, a bow is one who sends away.

You, in your essence, are the arrow,
the one who goes away.

Why should I be surprised
when, suddenly, you are not here?

123.

Every day, from inside your generosity,
you give me different love-shirts.

I am your Jacob. You are Joseph.

With these changing shirts
let me see again the way
I saw in pre-eternity.

 124.

It has been a long time
since my soul felt ecstatic.

There have been a lot of fingerpointing
critiques of this friendship.

Leaving the world will not be hard.
Leaving the path to where
you live, impossible.

125.

I say, How are you?
Do you feel happy or sad?

You say, Does anyone ever ask
the moon how it is? Or how
it came to be the moon?

No. It is just here, not-here,
luminous, darkened, circular,
crescent, always wholly itself.

 126.

When my heart begins to open
into words again, I know
that I will soon be accused,
because with every breath, with each new line
your presence comes here again.

My words can do nothing
but bring you back to life.

127.

There is a time in the making of wine
when must rises off and goes out across town
with a fragrance that wakes the heart.

That scent comes from the great soul-source
and returns to that, within each individual heart.

128.

It would be so fine if there were someone here
who had the power of silent understanding,
who without speaking or waiting for others to,
without explaining or asking questions, yet
still, because of whose presence, blessings
arrive, like the owner of a vast melonfield, who
lets the delights of spring and summer come
naturally, like the melons of the Kunduz Valley,
to please a radiant, long-expected guest.

129.

You cannot get away from people
by making your hearing sharp, by being more alert.

Nor can you escape yourself by being eloquent,
or by making a living from selling those words.

Neither way will bring you freedom
from people or from yourself.
Only silence does that.

130.

You died trying to undo your knots.
You are living now,
but you feel you are dying in separation.
Remember that you were *born from union*.

You are thirsty, yet you sleep
on the bank of a freshwater lake.

Bowl in hand, you sit begging,
when under the ground you sit on,
ancient treasure is buried. Just *here*.

131.

I do not say much,
because I cannot put in words anything true
about you. You are *something within*
that keeps me happy.

But I cannot put my finger
on what you are, or who.

132.

Some people say, "Come down into the orchard.
Things change there under the trees.
Laughter comes easily. . . . No noise of crows."

But I have one inside my heart
who creates all color, the dyer of dyers.
From one black crow feather,
we make many orchards.

133.

Night.   Night.   Let it be black night.
Let the sun go down in a well like Joseph.

So he gets sold to a caravan
going by on the way to Egypt.

Say the thief this time
is a nightpatrolman,
a master of the heart.

Let this story happen
as it must, again and again.

134.

The deepest love is one with many difficulties.
Somebody who avoids those is not a real lover.
It takes great courage to do the dance of lovers.

A moment comes when love touches the soul.
Then you must give up your life.

135.

I hear doves making the soft
sad music that we know in our lives.

coo-coo-coo

On her high branch I tell her,
Keep singing your beautiful song.
Keep on.

 136.

You have opened a secret tonight
that is the night itself, where black,
dervish-outcast crows dissolve into
joy, gone to fly with the white falcon.

137.

You are an ordinary human being.
That simplicity is better
than all existence.

Overcome with loss,
your drowning is a glory.

You say, *Everything here is dust.*
But the angels envy your dust.

138.

On a wild, unbroken horse,
in the middle of a desert plain.
The horse has torn away the reins,
running one way then another,
like a bird who has escaped the snare.

What is this horse I ride?
Where is it going?

139.

Regarding love, people see me
as a clear-eyed observer.

They put me in front of the assembly
to hear what I have to say *about love.*

Then winter comes, and I have nothing
made of sheepskin to wear with the wool side
against my shirt, no protection, even though
in every town I visit, someone has made
for me a good animal-skin overcoat.

Nothing helps this chill I feel.

 140.

They say that love begins in storm
and ends in a calm.
They say that love is, at its core, peace.

Soul is the still bottom stone
in a mill. The always-moving body
is uppermost, the turning one.

141.

Love is an ocean without a floor, or an edge,
a drop suspended with all souls drowning in it.

Love is among the most ancient secrets,
containing one small bit of hope.

The rest is awe in the presence
of the one loved.

142.

Look at the pile of you there
sleeping draped over each other,
a crowd. Your body, your personality,
your mind, spirit, voice, ego, your writing style.

Do you need a companion to walk with?
Sound the reveille.

Don't keep stepping over
those dozing relatives.
Wake them all!

143.

Do not call the lover a *lunatic*.
Do not say your friend is a *stranger,*
who shares his cloak with you
on cold nights traveling.

Do not call the ocean we swim in
a cup. That one knows the Name,
even if you do not. Try not to lie.

144.

For a long time I stood delighted
in the mud. Then someone suddenly
cut me away, and someone else
carved nine careful wounds
in my beheaded form, the reed
that is now a flute.

Now you will understand why
I might cry out awhile for all
that has happened to me.

145.

You that live in my heart,
in the opening happening there,
there is no one like you anywhere.
I will not go out looking.

Those I tell about you say,
No, there is no such.

But don't you also say *No.*
I have no way to go
away from you.

146.

There is no one who is not in love.
No one without this ache, this longing
rising from the tip of a black
thread in the dark.

You do not see it, but it *is* there.

147.

Any soul with an image of you
inside it will stay clear and flowing.

The new moon appears as a very thin
crescent edge, yet that slender arc
becomes a circular perfection.

148.

One day, drinking wine at your tavern,
I leave my mud-body behind.

I see that the whole world is ecstatic
because of your presence here
in this tavern, and that I have become
like I am, prosperous and dirt-poor,
hilarious and hungover-sad, exhausted,
because of this tavern place and what
flows through it, you and the wine.

149.

The heart is a garden, hidden away,
with beautiful trees.

It takes hundreds of different forms,
but it is always the same.

The heart is an ocean, all around us,
without bottom or shore.

Waves of it keep moving
inside each, in various ways.

150.

At the moment of death
when your soul is finished with your body,
it leaves it in the earth
like clothes that you have worn out.

Then the soul makes a new light-body
out of the source it comes from.

151.

I come to the beloved in an offhand,
careless mood. *Go away.*
You are drunk.

No, I'm not. Open the door.

However you are, you are,
self-being being a form
of drunkenness.

 152.

When the dawn of great friendship
begins to come up over us, the souls
of those then alive will begin to *fly.*

Human beings will be in a new place
where they can see the friend
without the distorting inconvenience of eyes.

153.

There is a dear speaker inside me
who makes fun of the legendary
lovers, Khusrow and Shirin.

Sometimes he makes me rush into action
while he remains still.

Other times he keeps me tame,
as he becomes fiercely quick.

154.

Spiraling up like a snake
spellbound in music, curling like hair,
I do not know what this circling is,
but I know that if I am not drawn
to be inside it, I am not alive.

155.

Let yourself sleep. Let worrying go,
the mind's jealousy, suspicion.
All that is a veil across the full moon
of the heart. Throw worry
in the river. Let it wash away.

 156.

If your hands cannot do work,
let your feet try. When your feet give out,
make up a song and start singing.

When there is nothing left that you can do,
go in where your thinking is,
the source of reason.

Keep on through all these ways
breathing praise and love.
In every moment, breathe adoration.

157.

Read one page of this book
and be drowned in bewilderment.
Study one heart-lesson,
and teachers from the other knowing
will come and sit down in your presence.

158.

My voice feels hoarse, caught,
awed in your presence.

I sound wounded with a hesitation
that can only fall down before you.

159.

For the old ones, being small
is no small thing. Childhood
comes out of a perfection.

When a father tells his child a story,
he knows that he is not a child.

 160.

On days of snow and mud it is good
to make *kashi*. Do you know why?

Learn something. Wet and moist mix together.
Wheat flour, honey, molasses, and hot melted butter
combine to then become the hard candy, *kashi*.

And so do we. Our days of snow and mud
become solid, so we can slowly
learn traction, balance.

161.

When eyes do not see the beauty,
do they make the beauty less?

What people say,
does that matter to a lover?

We move along this love-road
quickly, with agility in our step.

When one of us draws up lame,
do we all stop?

 162.

Someone not as light on his feet
as the soul is not a true lover.

Nor is one that does not stay close
to the moon, as Venus sometimes does.

Listen. This is true. Without wind,
flag-lions do not dance.

163.

Your existence and your nonexistence
are entirely *that*.

What makes you happy, what makes you cry,
all this is *the friend*.

But your *eyes* do not see the beauty.
Otherwise, you would realize that,
head to foot, you are *living inside*
the one you ask about.

164.

Love comes to me and enters
my blood, my veins, my skin.
Love empties the old self out
and fills me with the friend,
every aspect of my being,
body, soul, spirit.

The old name is still there,
but nothing else.

165.

As a lover, when I practice patience,
I set my clothes on fire,
and not only mine, everyone's.

When I cry out, my voice is burning,
and not only that. This whole world
burns, and nonexistence too.

166.

I love the soul that lets my soul
stay healthy, growing
like an orchard, a garden.

He brings symbols through me
to show the world.

Then at other times,
he clears my consciousness
to be transparent like himself.

167.

You are an inspired piece of writing,
a mirror reflecting the ultimate beauty.

Nothing in this world is outside of you.
When you desire something, anything,
look in yourself. You *are* what you long for.

168.

Candle, you may well imagine yourself
a good Sufi. You certainly have
the six qualities of purity: You get up
at night, face radiant, yet pale, humble.

That's three. Your heart is fiery (four),
grieving (five), and strikingly awake (six).

169.

Whichever way I bow, I bow to you.
All six directions, and more, are you.

Garden, rose, nightingale, music,
those are just synonyms for you.

170.

I am not this one you see. If I were that *me*
you do not see, even for a moment,
I would stir up this dust-particle world.
I would mix and confuse it together.

If I were that *me,* who has uprooted
his heart from any personal limits,
I would be like a tree lifted out
from the ground with roots exposed
to the air like its limbs and leaves.

171.

I see love running alone, naked,
bodiless, on a wide desert plain.

My heart recognizes the grandeur there
and says to itself, *When I escape from
form, I will play love-games with that.*

172.

For one like you, love is beauty
and eloquence and generosity.

For one looking for this love,
there is no half-way. Nothing stingy
happens when a beautiful one
meets a beautiful one.

173.

They say that love is an empty word,
a noise we make. What a lie.

They say that love is naïve,
unrealistic. Another lie.

For us the great communion is within,
here, but they point upward. *Love
will come there.* Not so.

They say, *Don't trust the friend.*
They say, *There is no coming back
after separation.* Big lies.

They say the excitement of love
is not part of soul-growth.

They say all this talk of love
is sentimental mysticism.
Those are the worst lies.

174.

The friend wonders,

How long shall we stay apart like this,
looking at each other?

I am the one who helps.
Love is the helpless one.

What is an image of the soul?

A small child in the cradle.

What does the heart look like?

A stranger from another country,
wandering here as a beggar.

175.

The time has gone
when I could be content
within your love.

And because of your love
I cannot remember you.

Cause and effect have no meaning,
empty air. A mud foundation
cannot be laid on ocean waves.

176.

You say, How are you?

This day moves along well enough.
Like the sun, I keep tearing and sewing cloth,
tearing evenly and sewing the seam
of sun across the sky.

Since I have seen your face, I burn
with color like the wild rue. Wild rue.

177.

One who has a friend of water and clay
has one day of union.
That's how it goes in the body.

One who has a friend in the spirit,
in the heart, has a king,
an outlandish, rare friend like you.

178.

Qur'an 57:4. The good news comes:
He is with you wherever you are.

Bits of firelight from that
appear in your heart.

You grieve because you do not know
who you are, but when you do know,
you fill with those lightpoint sparks.

179.

My chest is full and breathing
in your writing school, but the doctor says
that I have caught a fever from you.

So I have given up what
he told me to, all but the kindness
and the wild soul fury of your presence.

180.

We are the lazy lovers, lying
on our sides in the grass, talking, napping.

Generosity and grace have fitted the earth
under us with saddles, strong horses,
and a well-made wagon,
so that *we* can be carried along this way
in our sleep, in our laziness.

We are like those young men and their dog,
the cave companions, who slept
joyfully for centuries.

181.

The friend says, I am beautiful,
so make yourself beautiful.
Live in this friendship.

If you want to be a source of gemstones,
let your chest become the ocean.

 182.

The friend says, let the beauty
of this friendship be your beauty.

The source of sweetness is a nowhere.
Make yourself a place to live
there where there is no *where*.

183.

We wish we could see those
who are blessed. Others wish this too.

Now it happens that by our playfulness
and laughter our longing has removed
all our manners, every conventional practice,
and whatever else there was inside of us.

 184.

This one wanders the night-town
because of a different wine.

The jug he drank from is empty
and spinning on top of his head.

You righteous, religious police,
do not scold this friend of mine,

because the more you talk,
the drunker he becomes.

185.

Even in hell, if you are with me,
I would not want to leave.

And if I find myself in heaven
without you, those wide fields will
be confining to my breathing-heart.

186.

The one who looked down at us
from the roof yesterday, that one
is a spirit, someone radiantly inward.

Anyone who has lived without knowing
a face like that has not lived.

If you claim to be awake,
without knowing such a being,
it is proof that you are not.

187.

Every house without a lamp, my friend,
is a prison. Do not call it a garden.

Every bird that hears the drum,
Come back, is not a falcon.

Sometimes a crow lights there
and pretends to be the king's falcon.

 188.

Do not presume the earth
around you, this world, do not
think all this is unconscious.

It is rather like a rabbit, awake
with eyes half-closed,
like a pot of water
when a thousand tiny bubbles
begin to come up to tell
the cook it is about to boil.

189.

Love came and said
that I should be only with it,
that I should avoid being
sensible, steady, intellectual.

So love and I kept visiting,
back and forth, until now.
I did not go home.

I live here now, inside
this new annihilation.

 190.

A warm, rainy day—this is how
it feels when friends get together.

Friend refreshes friend then,
as flowers do each other,
in a spring rain.

191.

We are not in charge of anything,
just wandering through, causing trouble.

Of all those staying in this caravanserai,
I am the least respectable.

No. None of that is true.
We are a brush in the hand of the mystery
that is painting this soul-making universe.

As *that,* we do not know where we are,
or what we are doing in this moment.

192.

I say to my heart, *Not again,*
not a new love, all that suffering.

The friend, who is also my heart, says,
I bring you new wonders and beauty.
This hesitation is your pride.

193.

Something looks inside
and outside at once.

That *something* has great skill
at seeing how it is with those
who are lost in love.

Now look at all these eyes.
How do *they* see, and *who*
is looking out?

194.

Every floating bit of dust
close around us here and out over
the high desert, all these are just
as distracted and amazed as we are.

Each of us, whether personally happy
or sad, feels the incomparable joy
of the great sun there living inside us.

195.

NOW. The time for discipline has come.
Observe Ramadan. For a few days
hold back even from mentioning
the bowl for eating hot lentil soup,
the jar for keeping springwater cool.

Wander this empty tablecloth of sky,
begging. Let the cotton of the soul
loosen from the pod that holds it.

196.

Even though you cannot see the end—
it may be there is no end—still,
start out on whatever is your way.

Watching others on the way
is how a coward lives his life.

This way is for someone with heart,
a true human being who has moved beyond
what the body fears and what the body wants.

197.

I touch the hem of your robe,
and now I cannot let go. Your wine
will not leave my brain.

You say, *Appear as you are.*

But if I did, this physical world
would not contain me.

 198.

I said, *My heart is the instrument I play,
like a cello tuned to my voice.*

So when I found that my heart
had found another, I kept repeating,
foolishly, *But that's* my *friend.*

199.

Do not say that no one is truly on the Way,
that no one now is Christlike,
that no one has *really* dissolved their ego,
just because you haven't.

Others may well have.

200.

My ecstatic heart adores this tavern.
I offer up my soul too for a cup
of wine from here, a taste of spirit.

By giving both heart and soul
to this friendship, I can escape
some of the grief of being human.

201.

This is a day for running out
on the field like a polo ball. Stay well
in front of the polo stick today.

Time to move quickly.
Do not sit back with those
confused about what to do.

This is the resurrection, my soul.
Roll out onto the field of play.

202.

The inner one that was your companion
became a stranger.

The sensible doctor became
wholly unpredictable.

We know that kings often
hide their treasure in ruins,
but this field of rubble is here
because of its great value.

203.

Your friends, the beloveds,
all live within the circle of BE!

Kun fa-yakun. Be and it is.
Qur'an 2:117. The heart is
a point of union—moreso
than even the sky.

As it was with Muhammad as a child,
when there was one speck of pain left
in his heart that two angels came
and washed away. When that dissolves
in *you,* you will find a way of being
outside the circle of this existence.

204.

Sometimes I call you *wine,* sometimes *cup.*
Sometimes *refined gold,* sometimes
crude silver mixed with other alloys.

Sometimes you are *seed, quarry, trap.*
Why say all these names?
So I won't say your real one.

205.

My mind, my head, you are
synapse within synapse within
reasonable, measured synapses.

Body, you are wonders set within wonders,
threaded through by other wonders.

My heart, your desire hides within
a longing within a deep core of love.

Soul, your joy lives within yourself,
within another joy within the whole,
which is also a great joy.

206.

Everyone wants union with you.
The desiring is universal. Does anyone reach?

Someone who does will feel a deep peace.
Those who do not, feel restless,
so full of longing that it is almost
as if the *not-finding* is enough.

207.

If you become a lover of that face,
the one who rules the Kingdom of Rum,
you may have some hope of being truly alive.

Do not mention separation here.
Worry instead that you may not be
participating in this conversation.

 208.

Sometimes, a separation that wants
to burn up this world and leave.

Other times, the inward joy of union.
We feel them both.

How odd and sad it is
that on the white tablet where
everything has already happened,
it says, *This on one day.*
That on another.

209.

Now that your kindness has won out,
this is how it is: no meanspirited
people anywhere. The worries
about *more and less* dissolve.

Inside this majesty everyone
becomes a king, in this country
that has no beggars, just kings.

210.

I am the guest of music.
You are the life of these friends,
the soul of this music,
swaying ocean-center.

Let this wide music-field
be filled with your being.

211.

Every day the sun girds up, pulls its belt tight,
and gets ready to die.
The moon, forlorn and heart-empty,
the cypress and the rose, so strong and delicate,
they are all getting ready, as I am,
to die within you.

 212.

As a young child I went eagerly to school
and loved listening to the teacher.

Growing up, I was so happy
to see my friends' faces.

But something different is happening
here further along in my story.

I came in visible form, a cloud.
Now I leave invisibly, as wind.

213.

When I step over into death,
I will give a great shout
into nonexistence,

so that the emptiness itself
will be astonished, saying,

Nowhere in that world or this
have I seen someone so wild
in their love for what is,
and what is not.

214.

This is how the heart sounds.
Do not change the melody,
this now, you and I, here together.
Let this being with each
other be heart-sound.

215.

I am so near my friend,
not even soul has such nearness.

This is way beyond remembering.
Memory is for *thinking about*
someone absent. Forget memory.

216.

Evening already, and look at us,
disheveled in a love-muddle.

In an ocean, no shore visible,
sailing along at night, thick fog.

It's the ocean of God we
move through, such grace.

217.

I have filled all the paper made in Egypt,
and all that made in Baghdad too,
with this longing-talk poetry.

It must be that I must have forgotten
how an hour of actual friendship,
being in your presence for just that long,
is worth a world of verbal imaginations.

Dear one, let this living
be what we offer up.

Soul Fury

Excerpts from
The Sayings of Shams Tabriz

Introduction: Shams Tabriz

 **SOUL FURY**

There is an ornery, fierce, harsh intensity in some human beings that is difficult to define. Shams Tabriz calls it soul fury. He feels that it *must* find some form of expression that is honest and clear and immediate. That expression may be different in each case. It is the source of action. It moves away from language and books and toward "walking out and doing things." It brings with it strength, originality, spontaneity, and a playfulness that is often disguised as a wild fluidity of mind.

Wholly unpredictable. The subject can change in an instant.

WHO IS SHAMS?

It was a complex question when Rumi and Shams met 767 years ago, and Shams' identity is still an enigma. In March 2005, I was in Herat in western Afghanistan. The great *Masnavi* scholar Omani Chisti lives there. He was over ninety at the time. He has been teaching Rumi's masterpiece for seventy-five years. I had the honor and great good fortune of having tea with him one afternoon. Sitting there in his house, I leaned my shoulder against his and said, "Who is Shams?" He answered quickly. "Shams is the doctor who comes when you hurt enough. In the thirteenth century, the longing was intense enough. He came. Now it is not strong enough." I told him, "I came to Afghanistan to hear you say that." I am not a scholar, but the U.S. State Department sent me as the first speaker to go there in twenty-five years, to celebrate the fact that Afghanistan and this country share a love for Rumi, who was born near Balkh in northern Afghanistan.

The incandescent friendship of Rumi and Shams has always been difficult to fathom. Rumi called a collection of poems *The Works of Shams Tabriz,* implying that without Shams the poetry would not exist. In the stories of their meeting are moments of mystical astonishment, and throughout their three years together and afterward, each continued to be amazed by newly revealed depths in the other's being. The openings kept opening. Their time together became continuous *sohbet* (mystical conversation) with each other, with those around them, with the universe. Annemarie Schimmel said that what we come to understand from reading Shams' words is that he is "an embodiment of the living presence of God." The friendship of Rumi and Shams is one of the great mysteries. Perhaps it cannot be described or put into words at all. It can only be lived. With Rumi and Shams we get a full picture of the human/divine complexity, and the continuous creativity that is possible within it.

Shams Tabriz is a chef of consciousness. He likes to stir things up, to keep the situation fluid and tasty. He is playfully, relentlessly experimental with circumstances and consciousness. When Schimmel read Chittick's manuscript, she described the Shams that appeared out of that text as "raucous and sober, outspoken and subtle, harsh and gentle, learned and irreverent."* Chittick himself speaks of Shams as astonishing, jocular, colloquial, authentic, outlandish, repetitive, incoherent, confrontational. I would add my own adjectives: raw, innocent, disruptive, explosive, goofy, philosophical, whole, myriad,

---

* William Chittick, *Me and Rumi: The Autobiography of Shams-i Tabrizi* (Louisville, KY: Fons Vitae, 2004), x.

combative. He is a maddening, amazing human being. Others will have to throw their own scattershot language at this vivid, protean man. He defies definition.

With Shams, something unusually powerful has been embodied (his spirit, his soul fury), and something else (his form, his personality) is both mightily enjoying the embodiment and chafing at the constriction. In quatrain 88, Rumi records him as saying, "Are you trying to put me in that, in a poem? No house built in that way will ever hold me!" But Shams himself makes the famous formulation about Rumi's poetry, that it was written in three ways, three scripts. "One that he could read and only he, one that he and everyone else could read, and one that neither he nor anyone else could read. *I am that third script.*" Shams insists on being unreadable, inscrutable, misunderstood, unlovable, and some would say, he succeeds in being all these things and more besides. He's irresistible. Shams lives in the wild part of the psyche, to use Gary Snyder's divisions of the regions of consciousness into *tame* and *wild*. He is the nourishing wilderness, a healthy balance for Rumi's astonishingly rich caravan, an entire Silk Road of stories, myth, and imagery. Their friendship is a great gift to the world.

Some people are more intensely honest, more spontaneous, more fiery and original in the way they live and love. Shams is one of those. He moves along inside some powerful questions. Is there someone who can endure my presence? Is there a friend for me? That question got an answer: *Jelaluddin of Konya*. Shams also was looking for a way to live with both severe discipline and more complete freedom for his soul's vital *fury,* which must be given room to range.

Robert Bly's intuitive sense of Shams in the 1980s was that he was "a wild meditator, Thoreau times five hundred, Cervantes times fifty, Dostoyevsky times ten." Bly sensed a ferocious intelligence coming through the stories we have about Shams, or perhaps he felt it coming through Rumi's poems, at least five hundred of which end by mentioning or addressing Shams directly. Bly has always been brilliant at sensing how deep being filters through a text. He has also said that the reason Rumi is so popular now in the West is that the ecstatic passages were expunged from the New Testament, and so from Christianity, with the Council of Nicea in 326 AD, and that Rumi is reminding us of, and taking us back into, that region.

Shams Tabriz speaks from somewhere else. His state is much more practical, more activist. He wants his work to be *useful* in dissolving the ego, to help people be free—never smug or comfortable or congenial, which are all forms of hypocrisy. Shams lives in a fierce clarity. He is harsh with his friends, and especially with Rumi. He wants them to be more real, truer than they have been, not stuck in any teacher-student business or borrowed book-knowledge. He wants them not to lie or be false to themselves or others. One of his favorite words is *hypocrisy*. A strong word to use about your deepest soul friend and how he presents himself in the world. Shams' second-favorite word might be *boredom*. He most definitely does get bored.

As a human being, Shams, I feel, is in the area of Gurdjieff, Bodhidharma, Rinzai, Osho, Jonathan Swift, Dostoyevsky, Mark Twain, Nietzsche, Robert Bly, Pascal, Bawa Muhaiyaddeen, Thoreau, Cervantes, Henri Corbin, Socrates, Brando—here I drift into the ecstasy of list-making—Sophocles, Galway Kinnell, D. H. Lawrence, Picasso, Van Gogh, John Cage, Beethoven, Emerson, Henry Miller, Oscar Wilde, Timothy Leary, Herman Melville, Nabokov, Patrick Kavanagh, Bashō, James Joyce, Jim Morrison, Ishmael Reed, Richard Wright, Dionysus, Zarathustra, Hanshan, Bill Murray, Bernard Shaw, Mauvine Betch (the beachlady), Black Elk, Thomas Hardy, Mary Oliver, Plotinus, Gary Snyder, Franz Wright and his father James, William Blake, Hafez, Coleridge, Emily Dickinson, Janis Joplin, Georgia O'Keefe, Susan Sontag, Gertrude Stein, Willa Cather, Ibsen, Knut Hamsun, Samuel Beckett, Robert Hass, Hieronymous Bosch, Woody Allen, Stravinsky, Cormac McCarthy, Walt Whitman, Van Morrison, Hakim Sanai and his teacher Lai-Khur, James Hillman, Kharraqani, Mark, Meister Eckhardt, Philip Levine, Milarepa, Lorca, Machado, Vallejo,

Chuang-tzu, Nanao Sakaki, Carl Jung, Shirdi Sai Baba with his brick, and my friend Ed Hicks. There are many others that I am forgetting—Lao Tze, William Stafford, Dōgen, Ramakrishna, and others that I don't know about yet. Throughout my life I have felt excited and nourished by finding the new forms that this energy, the soul fury creativity, takes.

So what to make of this crazed crowd of names? Nothing. They are magnificent individuals who don't care about belonging to any tradition. And they don't want followers. Shams Tabriz is one of those. These are iconoclastic, crowd-dispersing loners. They come, they do their work, and they leave. We get to share the amazing, elusive, indefinable wealth of their being here. As Rumi says in #203:

> Your friends, the beloveds,
> all live within the circle of BE!

Sufis say that every person is capable of becoming a True Human Being, an *insan kamil* in Arabic, and that to speak and act from that place is wildly provocative to all conventional notions. It is also charismatic, transformative, and *necessary* for human evolution. How does one know when that is happening in oneself or in someone else? That is one of the secrets. It is different in every person. Comparisons are of no use. I feel as if

I have been on the lookout, on the prowl, for these people since I was twelve. Someone truly and wildly alive, free. I feel that I can recognize it, in people, in paintings, in writing, as a kind of originality, an authenticity of self. Maybe it is so elusive and undefinable because it truly *must be lived*. It is each person's own soul, the eternal self, the friend we long for, long to meet, to become. The one who goes to the door from inside, the one who comes to the door from outside, the one who knocks, and the merging of identities in the opening.

Shams is ferocious about protecting his privacy. He will meet with someone only if he feels a strong heart-and-soul connection. Shams claims to be much more concerned than Rumi about practical matters. He says Rumi has a compassionate vision, but he himself actually gets out and does something to help. He *acts*. He grabs people by the seat of their pants and lifts them out of harm. What Shams often seems to be doing in these passages is accusing Rumi of placating his students. He says that Rumi pleases, appeases, consoles those around him. He avoids confrontation, and so is not completely truthful. What Shams learns from Rumi is the pleasure of hearing the *language* of transcendent states. Before he met Rumi, he had been unaware of the delight of the ecstatic way and the language that can come out of that. (See the end of #5, page 155.)

Shams is not a poet. He is deeply suspicious of language. He feels that words cannot say who we are in any essential way. But then again, he does like to know where language comes from and where it's going. He hates it when he doesn't know the internal source, or when the source is somewhere other than it seems to be. I would claim also that Shams is *radically interested* in language, in the mystery of words and how they *can* contain the soul's essential force. As he said, Rumi's poetry somehow embodied *him* on a deep level. But what does that mean? I have arranged these excerpts of Shams' as a long free-verse poem, like an unruly descendant of Whitman's *Song of Myself.* I have numbered the sections for convenience, but maybe they should be more airy and expandable, innumerable.

When I first came to Rumi's poetry, in 1976, I felt that I was drawn by the mystery of Shams Tabriz. Years later, I had a dream about just that. I was being directed into a cave by my friend, the poet Galway Kinnell. Above the cave's mouth were words, in flame-letters, RASA SHAMSI TABRIZ. The Essence of Shams Tabriz. I entered the cave and came to a great vertical abyss. Along the sides of it at irregular intervals were niches where meditators were seated. The atmosphere was profoundly inward. It was the most sacred place I have ever experienced, in dream or out. At the level where I came in, there was a flat place with a rough, square, low wooden chair facing the abyss. No one was sitting in it. In the dream I considered it Shams' seat. I sat down on the cave floor to the left of the chair. Someone else would sit on the right. That was the entire dream, still vivid in my memory. I am fascinated by such numinous dreams. I feel as if this one gives a wordless feeling-tone, something of the nature of Shams' communal depth.

❋ THE SAYINGS OF SHAMS TABRIZ

The Sayings of Shams Tabriz has gone through many transformations as it has come down to us over the last eight centuries. Rumi and Shams were together in Konya for about three years, 1244–47. Whenever they talked together, someone in the circle, or more than one, would take notes. These notes were preserved in various learning communities around Turkey. They circulated and were copied and recopied. Later those collections of notes were also kept in libraries. This great ragged assemblage was never systematically collected or organized. In the 1970s Mohammad-Ali Movahhed began to do that work. He spent years poring over the disjointed, confusing texts. Then in 1977 he published the first of two volumes in Tehran, in Persian. The second came out in 1990. Total page count, about 550 pages.

Six ancient manuscripts have been preserved that record these random notes, discourses, and conversations of Shams with Rumi and various others. Movahhed thinks some of the more coherent passages were dictated by Shams directly to a single scribe. He does not claim to have found an order to the materials. William Chittick's work began in September 2001. He organized the notes into three sections—"My Years without Mevlana," "My Path to God," and "My Time with Mevlana." The final result came out in 2004: *Me and Rumi: The Autobiography of Shamsi Tabrizi.* Chittick says that some passages are "surprisingly colloquial," earthy. Shams loves to fool around, joking, leaving important things out, often changing tack. He is often abrupt and irrational. However, the great Persian scholar Furuzanfar considered Shams' *Sayings* as one of the great treasures of Persian literature, written in language both simple and profoundly moving, and requiring "several contemplative re-readings."

OTHER OBSERVATIONS

Shams' sentences do not proceed logically. Maybe he has his own illogical or numinous structure. I don't know.

Accusations of hypocrisy, boredom, and disgust with the teacher-student thing—these are strategies that Shams uses to get to the truth and reveal one's true identity. He hates congeniality, with its phony pretension of closeness. He also is suspicious of the ecstatic, and of what he sometimes calls *the presence.*

Shams is *not* interested in separating the transcendent (the spiritual) from the bodily, the physical. His stories often include basic bodily functions—farting, peeing, all that. He is not polite by any standard.

Shams knows that something needs to "come forth" from the psyche, and he tries to help that happen. If, as Omani Chisti told me, "Shams is a doctor," then he often heals with bitter medicine. He challenges your happiness, in whatever form that might take—ecstasy, complacency, peace, casual ease, conventional religiosity. He stirs things up by questioning your sense of your own holiness. He does not trust anything that consoles and makes nice. He wants your *soul fury* to be cleanly and vividly apparent.

Shams also does not seem to have had much use for vegetables, or fruit, or nuts, or desserts of any kind. He is more stern with kids in kindergarten than any educationist nowadays would be (see #32). He would ask a lot of a five-year-old. He feels that children should be given very early on a definite regimen for eating and drinking, so that they learn discipline and feel the strength of having that.

Shams talks about the small-mindedness of reading from one's own "personal book," by which he means, in part, the habit of continually finding fault with others or with life in general—the complaining mode.

Among many confounding things that Shams says is this: "I have no connection to suffering. Suffering comes from existence, and I have no existence" (#28). He may mean that he is *one* with existence and with spirit. Whatever he means, it is a mystery, and it feels true.

Shams claims in #24 to be able to dissolve a personality with all its ecstasy, its visions, its language, its highs and lows. He says he can eradicate all those illusions from a person by giving that person his own *awe and emptiness*—presumably, just by the force of his being near the man.

We don't know much, for sure, about Shams' teachers. A few stories have come down. When he was still a boy, he spent time with a man who liked to whirl him around in a "meditative dance." We don't know the name of this ecstatic teacher, maybe Sheikh Sallebaf (the wicker-worker). Shams says he felt with this master like a captive bird or a piece of bread being torn apart by a powerful young man who had not eaten for three days. Evidently, Shams was too young for what Sallebaf had to give. When the teacher left Shams, he said, "Put him off to the side until he catches fire himself." Another of Shams' early teachers, Kho'l, is also said to have left him, commenting, "God has created you just as you are, and I can't make any creatures of God ugly. I see a very noble jewel here. I cannot write on such a jewel."*

❈ THE DANGEROUS TRUTH

Another insight attributed to Shams has come down through the oral tradition:

> The Kaaba is at the center of the world. If you take
>   it away,
> if you lift it up and out of this world, you will see
>   that everyone
> is praying, five times a day, as a way of honoring
> the soul of everyone else.

This may be the core of the *dangerous truth* (#9, #18, #19) that Shams keeps threatening to speak but withholding. He suggests here that if you take away the icons of religion, you will be

---

* These stories about Shams' teachers are told in Franklin D. Lewis' *Rumi: Past and Present, East and West* (London: Oneworld, 2000), 145.

left with the core of what is truly sacred, which is how human beings recognize the soul in one another: friendship, compassionate insight, love, spirit, the beauty of companions. This is a dangerous (and radiant) truth, in any age, implying nothing less than the setting aside of *all* religious traditions. The Kaaba, Mecca, the Qur'an, the Bible, the Cross, the eucharist, the cathedrals, Jerusalem, all the Jewish traditions and scriptures, the Hindu gods and temples, the Buddha, the sutras, all the holy statues, shamanic drawings, all the holy paraphernalia that we love. Or it may be some truth that is beyond my ability to say or see.

Hopefully, from the following excerpts, one can get a more experiential sense of what Shams means by the cleansing power of *soul fury*.

Soul Fury

1.

Everybody is in love with this word, *Bravo!*
They spend their lives trying to hear it called out
    to them.
Bravo! Bravo!

2.

Crowing comes from the rooster.
Morning comes from God.

3.

All this attention to teachers and disciples, to learning,
    to principles and branches of theology, all this is a
    covering for the true way. It hides it.
First, you must become disgusted with all that. Raise
    your hand and say,
La illahha Illallahu. The mystery of the *zikr.* Everything
    is God.
This is a sacred universe. Live in it.

4.

The purpose of a story is not to hold your attention,
but to put you back doing your work, inner and outer.

A story is not for presenting some explicit meaning,
and it is not for anyone's entertainment.

5.

I have no special quality such that anything I might say
would be of any interest to Rumi.
That's not my work here.

One day I was growing bored with our talking.
I stopped one of my words as it came passing
    through me
and asked it, Where do you come from?

It said, God.

Where are you going?

To that great spirit, Rumi.
Then what am I doing here? I asked.
Why do you need to pass through me?
Use someone else. Use Imad, Arshad, Zayn Sadaqa.
Or else, start out here from me.
Stop using this body, this voice, as a passageway
from somewhere else to Rumi.

Now, though, with these words coming through,
I am *not* bored. I am, in fact, afraid
of doing something that would prevent them
from coming into being by way of me.
I would hate that.

How can we *judge* the great beings?
I do not include Muhammad in this question.
He is too vast and magnificent. God dipped
    Muhammad once
in the ocean of his generosity. Then lifted him out.

Droplets of light fell off. Each drop became a prophet.
Some leftover drops became saints.

There is no ranking those drops of light.
Muhammad is greater than any who came after.

Whatever insight has come to me has come
without my studying any of the sciences,
without any effort at all, without intellect.
It has all come because of the blessing
of being in Rumi's presence.

The first words I spoke to Rumi were, Why did not
    Bestami say,
How great is *Your* glory and We have not praised You
as You should be praised.

When Rumi heard these words in the clarity of his
    heart,
he became profoundly bewildered.

From my tasting the depth and secrecy of that state
    in him,
I have understood for the first time the pleasure
of language that rises out of such an ecstatic state.
I had not known, or felt, that pleasure before.

6.

I swear to God, I am not able to really know Rumi.
There is no false modesty or deception in my saying this.

Every day I learn things about his state and his actions
that were not there yesterday.

He is so alive and in motion that I cannot know him.
He has a beautiful face and presence, and he speaks
    eloquent words,
but do not be satisfied with those.
There is something beyond the form and the words,
beyond his face and the poetry.

Try to seek that *something* from him.

He has two sorts of expressions.
One is hypocrisy. The other is truthfulness.

Those who yearn to be in his presence, to sit
    with him—
many of those are saints, but they are wanting
to hear the public self, that which I am calling
his hypocrisy, not the core truth of his being.

That authentic essence—the great beings themselves,
Moses, David, Jesus, Muhammad,
these are gathering to take in that core of truth.

 7.

I am unable to know Rumi
because his words are like a blindfold.
I cannot see through them to his eyes
and know who he is.

His poetry is like that, a great joke really,
hilarious, a mask. A new kind of conjuring.

 8.

Let me say this clearly: Hypocrisy makes you ecstatic,
drunken with the *presence* you feel.
Truth makes you sad, discouraged, empty.

I said recently to one man, "You are just amazing.
There is no one like you in this generation."

He took my hand, "I have misjudged you." You see, last
    year I was not complimentary,
and he became my enemy. It's very odd. To live
    congenially with others,
you must be something you are not. Live then
    hypocritically,
if you want to get along with others. When you start
    to tell
what is really in your heart, you have to go to the
    mountains or to a desert.
There is no way to stay in community if you try to say
    the truth.

 9.

I have said that these words of mine are half hypocrisy.
If I were to say the full truth, everybody in this
    community would want to kill me.
You could not do it, though. Your aggression would
    point back on yourselves.
Try it and see.

10.

I told Rumi that my first requirement in this friendship
    with him
was that I should act *with* him the same
as I would if I were alone.

For example, when I am alone, I pee. I take a shit.
The body is a way to get around, a mount, a horse.
It eats fodder. It breaks wind. It pees.

You say all this does not matter.
I say it does.

11.

If you feel some hesitation, some fear about eating
    something,
or going somewhere, or doing something, don't eat it!
Don't go there! Don't do it!

12.

If sometimes I put on clothes that are torn and dirty,
that is intentional, a decision I make.

God, with me, is gentle, grace on top of grace. Within
   myself,
though, I move from being loving to being angry
and severe. Sometimes a harsh approach
feels more alive, truer. I get very bored
with too much gentleness.

 13.

Rumi has said many times
that he is more compassionate, more sympathetic with
   people than I am.

He is so happy in his ecstatic state
that when someone falls in deep water or into a fire, or
   into hell,
Rumi holds his chin in his hand and gazes at the
   situation
with kind eyes. He does not jump into the water or
   the fire.
He does not go down into hell. He gazes with kindness.

I have that gaze too, but I also grab the one in danger
by the seat of his pants and pull him out.

"Come on out, brother.
You too should be gazing this way."

What I do in these talks
is a way of grabbing and pulling you out
from wherever you have gotten yourself.

 14.

This is how it must be here with me.

Do not try to repeat what I have said here.
If someone asks about this meeting, say:
There was such communion.
The time together, the conversation,
was very nourishing for the soul,
but I cannot tell you exactly what he said.
Go and listen for yourself.

Never say to others what I say to you.
Instead, let this language *live inside* you.

15.

If you send someone to me, I will see who he is.

Then if I want to, I'll talk with him.

If not, I will stay quiet.

16.

Somebody says, Look at so-and-so. What a beautiful
   awareness!

I say, You claim to be *my* friend. Aren't you ashamed to
   say such a thing?

Do you mean he is *not* in an exalted state?

No. He is, very high, but anyone who is *my* friend
could not be satisfied with what he has.

17.

When you are connected by friendship to a great
   teacher,

you will have a permanent privacy about you.

Without actually sitting alone,

you will still be in a constant inward peace.

18.

There are many deep souls that I love internally, without
  showing it.

I sometimes don't let such love be known. It is there, but
  it does not take form.

Once or twice I have made it manifest by doing
  something while I was with them.

But they did not recognize the friendship I was offering,

nor did they accept their obligations in such
  companionship.

I do not allow their disregard to make my love for them
  grow cold.

On the other hand, when I let my love for Rumi open
  toward him,

the friendship always became greater, never less.

I cannot tell all the truth I know. If I did, if I said that
  all at once,

the whole city would throw me out. Even the very
  young and certainly the very old.

Rumi himself would join in to exile me. Would you like
  to know why?

Because, when he saw such extreme behavior, he would
  feel he had to join in

to help them realize the error of such excess. Then, in
   the midst of that,
he would see that I was going a different way, and he
   would turn and follow me.

 19.

When something must come out, I let it come,
even though everybody is telling me, *Don't say it!*
   Don't do it!

It might be a thousand years before these words can
   be heard
by those who are meant to hear them.

When Rumi is given inspired words, he speaks them
   with no concern
about how they will be received. He does not care about
   the effect,
one way or another. I am different. Since I was a child, I
   have been inspired
to use language in such a way that those who hear will
   be *delivered from themselves*
and move on. This is the way of an awakened master.

Some servants of this way are action people. They *do*
   their work.
Others are speakers. Their work is talking.
People need an active leader now more than one who
   uses language to lead.

However, this is how it has been decreed: When
   someone with the power of action
speaks, that speaking takes on the value and the power
   of acting. The words *act.*
Don't you feel it? How the things I say have strength?
   They go out in the world.
They put it right. It has never been my way to write
   anything down.

Since I don't do that, the words stay inside me, always
   changing,
showing me new faces. But all language is pretext,
something that is concealing something else,
and that *something* is the real, which has no covering,
which is pure beauty.

20.

I said to Rumi, "You go talk to these people. They are
     not getting what I say.
They want pretty metaphors. But I talk about essence.
And if I use a likeness, it is to something else essential.
     This is hard for them.
What I say gets covered over. But with you, nothing
     is hidden.
As you speak, they bow their heads and listen
like good dervishes." So he went.

21.

I do not need you to approve of me. I know my value.
Don't try to praise my soul's fury.
If you want to praise Rumi, watch and see what gives
     him peace.
Then make that happen. Do nothing to disturb him.
     The fact is,
whatever troubles my heart troubles his.
This talk of Rumi is not for my benefit. I know his state
     in myself.

22.

Ibrahim knows how we are together, Rumi and I.

When I say something, it's as if Rumi says it too.

Then it doesn't occur to him to say it as well, because
both of us have said it.

23.

In Baghdad a great master is taking on a forty-day
retreat.

On the night before New Year's he hears an inner
voice:

*We have given you the breath of Jesus. Come out and let
the people see.*

He wonders what this means. Some kind of a test?

The voice comes again, stronger. *Leave your hesitation
behind! Come out.*

*Go to many kinds of gatherings. We have given you the
breath of Jesus. Breathe it*

among the people. Still, he wants to consider this longer
in the clarity of his seclusion.

A third time. This time the voice is shouting: COME
OUT! He breaks his retreat.

It is the day of the festival. He's walking among
the crowds.

A candyseller has made little birds of sugar candy,
calling, *New Years' candy!*

He says to himself, I'll see about this breath of Jesus, and
calls to the candyman.

People wonder what the meditation master is doing. He
has no interest in candy.

He takes a birdshape from the tray and puts it on his
palm. He blows on it.

Immediately, it turns into a bird, feathers, wings, bright
eyes, intention, and flies away.

People gather closer. He does it again, again. And
once more.

The crowds are now prostrating on the ground around
him in awe and astonishment.

He feels oppressed by the attention. He sets out quickly
for the desert. They follow.

He turns on them: *I have work to do alone.* They keep
coming.

He prays, *Lord, what is this gift you have given that
envelops me with this crowd?*

Then an inspiration comes. *Do something to offend them.*
     So he farts.
The great master breaks wind loud and long. The
     people look at each other,
shake their heads, and leave, all but one.

The master sees the radiance of this one young man's
     need, the splendor of his soul.
Why didn't you leave with the others? The young
     man says,
*I was not blown in on the first wind of inspiration to let
     myself be blown out*
*by the second, and besides, the second is better. It gives peace
     to your blessed essence.*
That first wind, the charisma, *brought you a confined
     feeling.*
I prefer your second, crowd-dispersing, fart-wind.

 24.

These people, they live through this world; they live for
     it. They *are* this world.

Did you see how that man was sitting the other day,
    crushed,
because he was no longer the deputy? He had been
    fired.
He is still sitting that way today! And look at his
    clothes.
Oh, my time is over.

I will go and show him what he has forgotten:
the majesty of a human life, the soul fury of being alive.

I will give him my awe, my emptiness,
and that condition he is in now will dissolve.
Also his ecstasy, his visions, his careful watching,
his language, his highs and lows, all of that
will be gone, destroyed.

 25.

This Christian, I could listen to him talk all day.
I could listen for a hundred days and not get bored.
When someone gets boring and quarrelsome,
I set fire to his ego. That's the way to go deeper
with anyone. Burn the ego, what he identifies with.

Tear those buildings down! Let something better
    begin.

That Christian knows so many sciences, but nothing of
    his true value.
He works on something and imagines he brings that
    value into being.
He's working at the wrong place. He says, *Refresh me
    with the fragrance*
of the garden, which is good, what we say while cleaning
    the nostrils
in morning ablutions. He says it while cleaning
    his butt.
Right prayer, wrong hole.

 26.

Let me say again that you should not listen
    to the negative things people say about each other,
the gossip. For example, yesterday a man came to me
    and said that he had heard
what I had said about him. He confronted me. *Why did
    you say that?*

I have been with great souls. They liked me. They did not
     want me to leave.

I said, *Ask that with more courtesy, so I can answer.*

He said, *Let me sit for an hour, so my ego can calm down.*

I said, *Sit for two.*

He sat for one and came back. *I was admired. They called*
     me by beautiful titles.
Why is your opinion so different? Right now, say,
how would you describe me?
Give me a name.

If you have faith, I'll call you faithful. If not, I'll find some
     other word.
Now, if you want to continue this conversation without
     ego, do so.
Otherwise, I will not respond to you again.

27.

That guy, it was his own *asininity* that made him say
everybody from Tabriz is a jackass.
What could he possibly know about that city?

There are astonishing people there, among whom I am
   the least.
I am an ocean, but with them I am just a piece of
   driftwood
thrown up on shore. If I am like *this,* try to imagine
   what they are!

 28.

The reason for my talking so roughly to you
is so that your holding-back can come out
and not stay inside and fester.

As it is said, *He who torments you*
without having been tormented himself
is an idiot.

However, I also feel that there is great beauty
in tolerating and in showing mercy.
Grace is a kind of perfection.

I just have no connection to suffering.
Suffering comes from existence, and I have no
    existence,
or, say that my existence is all a kind of joy.
Why should I take on something external?
To hell with that! I throw it out of my house!

 29.

A man, very full of himself, comes to me
and demands that I tell him "the secrets."

I cannot do that, I tell him.
I speak about the inner life only to myself.

And I do not see myself in you.
I see someone else.

When anyone comes to meet you,
he comes in one of three ways: as a student,
as a companion, or as one of the great beings.

Which are you, would you say?
Did you not come here to meet me?

The visitor says, It is obvious how I have come to you.

Yes, it is, I say.

I see you there, and not myself.

I do not see myself in you.

 30.

I say this to those in my circle. This is my way. When
    someone comes to me,

I ask, "Will you speak or listen?" If he says he will
    speak, I listen continuously

for three days and three nights, unless, of course, he flees
    the premises,

and leaves me there alone. If he says he'll listen, I talk.

So I never have to put up with starting to talk

and then having him, or anyone, interrupt.

 31.

When I love someone, I turn toward him a stern side
    that some might call cruel.

If he accepts that from me, I become sweet and
    nourishing,

a morsel that he can take with him anywhere.

With a five-year-old child, if you act out of kindness, he
    will love you.

But there is a harsher way that is better.

What looks severe and unloving does the good work.

 32.

If you give a child to me, I will bring him up so that he
   has full control over his desires.

If he is hungry and wants an almond, I say, NO!
   Human beings eat bread!

With every so often a good meat stew. With a child I
   accept no foolishness about food.

Let him grow up learning discipline with eating and
   drinking.

That way, when he gets older, he can do what he wants.
   "Go ahead. Waste your life

if you want to." Such a child will grow healthy, full of
   energy,

and able to live within a regimen. He will almost seem
   to be a spirit.

The reason for such strictness is this: If a child grows up
   being indulged,

he will become self-absorbed and incapable of real
   soul-growth.

If you try to discipline him after he's grown, you'll have
   to kill him.
It's impossible, after a certain age. So there is a deep
   motive in my severity,
this rough treatment through the early years.

Of course, there are times when you put up with a
   child's nonsense.
Let his *soul fury* have its freedom. Don't teach children
   manners
for the sake of manners. When I see an adult doing that,
   I step in.
"Enough! Teach this courtesy to yourself!
Let the child grow in his own way."

 33.

When I am deeply with people,
it is with both severity *and* gentleness.
By myself, it is all kindness.

I don't want to explain myself about this.
Symbols are enough.
It is rude to offer explanations, but you have made me
bold and outrageous like this.

Water comes up out of the ground whole, as one thing,
the springhead, then it splits off into two streams,
with sometimes all the water in one branch, then all in
    the other,
then they empty, by turns, into each other.

Anyone who goes beyond this branching-off place
will find the headwaters, a depth.

Dive in, fully immersed,
and be free of all branchings,
those mental divisions and distinctions.

It is the same with trees. If you grab one branch,
it breaks, and you fall. But if you embrace the whole
tree, then all the branches are yours.

This is how it is with the beloved: In that presence
there is a kind of hashish, a danger, so that when people
    eat it,
they lose intelligence. They don't know where they are,
how they got here, or who the friend is.
They no longer feel their own *soul fury*.

34.

They ask someone, Do you want this cash
slapped in your hand now,
or the promise of money in the future?

He says, *Slap it here, and leave. Please.*

Always there is blessing in someone leaving.
He did not want the regret of losing that blessing,
the blessing that comes when someone leaves!

35.

Rumi says, "My sense of Shams has deepened.
He is looking for God in someone like me."

Rumi has it wrong. I am looking *inside God* for him.

36.

What can be said about the beauty of Damascus?
If it were not for Rumi, I would not have come back
from Aleppo and Damascus.

Even if Damascus were in ruins, that opening
   where people meet
would still be there. Deep friendship
is possible in such a place.

As for a field of knowing, the poet got it right.
Damascus is either heaven on earth,
or just below it.

I have to say the lines of a poem to understand them.
I must speak them outloud,
or I don't know what they mean.

 37.

Someone says, "I was on a ship. A jewel appears on the
   edge of the ocean,
a pearl of light. I look, and it almost takes away my
   sight.
I cover my eyes with my hands. . . ."

So you like wonders. You go around the world and
   inside yourself,
looking for amazing things. I have a suggestion.

There are things inside me that are beyond *all* that.
Come inside and see.

Another man imagines that my awareness is badly
    flawed.
He says, "Did you see what he did to my longing?"

What could you possibly know about the true
    search?
Buy some cotton and a spindle and sit there and spin
    all day.
That's enough for your *longing*.

The most powerful men hope to be able
to put two pots of water at my door.

 38.

There is a wool sack and a cotton sack and a pearl.
The wool sack says to the pearl,
"I am much larger than the cotton sack."

There is also a madman and a rational man.
The pearl says, "Let's ask the madman."

The madman has heard that there *is* a pearl. He says,
"Even if you fill both sacks with gold,
you still will not have enough to buy the pearl.
No one knows the price of the pearl.
Only the pearl can say that."

The rational man says, "Well. He's mad.
The pearl is unique in this world.
It will never have a price."

 39.

The attack on me by that big-bearded small man
is like the wool sack talking to the pearl.

What kind of wool exactly?
Foul-smelling wool.

I will not mix my words in his with an answer.
I will let his own words serve for that.

Jesus spoke in the manger.
Muhammad waited forty years.
Not from anything wrong. From his perfection.
He was the beloved.

They ask a servant whom he works for.
When they ask Muhammad that, he says,
I am the servant of God (19:30).

No one asks the king, Who are you?
Anyone always looking for faults
is reading a page from his own book.

If he were to read one line from the friend's page,
he would quit talking about what's wrong.

The calligraphy on your personal page
is ragged, bent, smeared, and full of suspicions.

Someone who reads only that personal page
has carved an image that he now is worshipping.

These holidays are like those images.
The days themselves are talking to you, saying,
Don't look for blessings from *us*.
We are hoping that *you* will instead bless us,
so that our day will lose its dayness, this hour
its hourliness, so that an inanimate object here
might come to life, into the animation that leads to
a consciousness that grows into God.

40.

If you cannot go with me on this way,
I have no response at all to that decision.

Likewise, my being separated from Rumi,
or my being reunited with him,
has nothing to do with my soul's joy.

That comes from within my own nature,
as does the pain I feel.

The difficulty that I have with living
has to do with my not being this or that,
or that or this, or *anything*.

41.

I am much happier sitting here with you talking
than somewhere like Tabriz, where I would be honored
with position and property, but they would not
    understand
my words. There is no greater delight
than this conversation here with you.

42.

It is not for me to ask you to go on a journey,
but I can travel myself, so that you can mature,
and your work can be accomplished.

Separation cooks.
Apart from me, you may reconsider. "Those
    commandments
and restrictions were nothing. So easy, compared
    to *this*."

But that is not the whole story. I am speaking in riddles,
hypocritically, looking to please both sides.
I could try to be more clear. First, what is the value
of this work that you are meant to do?

For that, I would make fifty journeys. It makes no
    difference
if I go to Damascus, or if I wander around Anatolia.
    Istanbul, Kaaba—
all the same. My traveling is for your growth,
    your work.

Now. Another question. Who is better,
the one cooked by union,
or the one perfected by separation?

They cannot be compared, really, the one with his
    eyes open,
seeing *what is*, and the one outside the veil, wondering
when he might be allowed in. There's no way to say.

 43.

When a poem comes in the middle of my talking,
I feel an opening. I begin to say the secret meanings.
Some people get quiet when they hear those.
Rumi himself gets overwhelmed sometimes that way.
Others get stunned by a lack of meaning.
None of this happens with me. I am rarely mute.

People have a right to object to anything I say.
These words come from a vast place.
They sound pretentious.

When Muhammad spoke the Qur'an, his words
came because they *had* to. There was an urgency,

a searching need. My speaking is not like that.
These words are from so high up,
if you try to look for the source, your hat will fall off.

People hear me and say, "He thinks he's so great."
That's like saying, "God thinks he's so great,"
which is true, certainly. What's wrong with truth?

 44.

I don't usually disagree with a saying of Muhammad,
    but here
is one that I do: *This world is a prison to a believer.*
I don't understand. I see no prison around me.

Though he did not say, *This world is a prison to a servant.*
Servants and *believers* are very different.

Prison I understand as a way of thinking,
an internal confinement. When that happens,
tell your friend how you feel, and be done with it.

Do not think, how can I be so smallminded
with this one I am close to?

Your soul knows all about everything,
whether you say anything or not.

 45.

I have never felt that this world is a prison.
All I see is an exalted sky, freedom.

If someone pisses on my hands, I immediately
   forgive him.
Thank you, sir. So, bravo for me!

You wonder why I hide myself away sometimes.
For much of my life, I did not know who I was.
Now I see. Such surprising beauty!
I am like a pearl one finds in a latrine,
down in the muck and the shit.

I had imagined myself to be free of all that.
Hardly. No. Not at all!

 46.

The work with dreams is full of danger,
but still I use those to teach.

47.

They will say, in coming years,
I wish I could have been there when Rumi was alive,
so we could have been his friends
and heard his words as he spoke them.

You have that very companionship now.
Do not waste this chance!

Look at him as the souls of the prophets are seeing him,
not with these skeptical faces you have.

48.

I love this—how we are together.
God has given me this friendship!

I was so bored with myself.
I wanted someone to talk with—
as a prayer rug turns to point,
someone to turn my face to.

Do you understand what I am saying
about boredom? You do. I have a friend now
who understands what I am saying!

49.

Studying books is a covering, a place to hide.
When you go into it, it's like choosing to go down in
    a well.
You will regret it, because eventually you will come
    to know
that you have kept yourself away from the real food.

You have been licking the pot. Words and the mind
are just busy-ness, distraction. They're the pot,
not the nourishment. That is somewhere else.

When Hakim Sanai was dying, he said something with
    just his breath,
very faintly. Those around him bent their heads close.
I turn away now from all I have said and written.
There is no core meaning in speech, and no speech in
    the core.
The life inside here cannot be spoken in words.

Sanai also said in his last days, *My knowing*
has reached to here: I know that I know nothing.

In his final moments you catch the fragrance of
    the man.

I have come to understand that all I said
and wrote, from beginning to end, is nothing.

 50.

What is this?
All we do and are, this friendship with God?

People say our lives are like
something we can walk into and out of.
Somewhere we sit down and listen for a while,
say a few things in response, and then leave.

Is this a soup kitchen where we get free nourishment?
We talk with friends, then go on our way.
Are we the homeless poor?

Is that an adequate image for the mystery
of this Friendship with the One?
The Oneness of all Creation. The turning galaxies,
this amazing earth, time, eternity?

Surely this is more than free soup
and casual conversation.

✣ 51.

Rumi is very subtle in his understanding of what is real,
and what is not. So in his presence
it is best to tell jokes.

We have been talking here about love, love.
We must talk instead about what we fear.

Take the story of the two men.
One of them has gold strapped around his waist
in a hidden belt.

The other knows about this. He's waiting for the man
to fall asleep. Everyone must sleep.

But the gold-carrying man stays half awake.
He sits up, napping lightly. He is one of those whose
    nature
is wakeful awareness. He can keep doing this
    indefinitely.

They reach the last way station of their travels together.
The potential thief gives up his plan.

He has taken too many precautions. He will protect
that gold no matter what. I'll joke with him instead.

Sir, why don't you fall asleep for a while?

Why should I do that?

So I can hit you on the head with this rock,
and while you are unconscious,
I can run off with that gold you have
strapped around your waist.

Very good. I understand who you are now.
I like you. I can sleep a calm and peaceful sleep.

And so he does.

Right now, out on a dangerous journey somewhere,
a man is sleeping.

One of God's friends has come along to wake him.
As it happens, the sleeper is already

in a deep communion with the one coming to
    wake him.

If I were to tell you the qualities of such a sleeper,
you would feel discouraged in your own life.
I won't say any more about this friendship
between those awake and those asleep.

Feel secure and encouraged within yourself.
There is hope.

 52.
What do I grieve about?

There are those who love this physical world,
those who love spirit, and those who *live inside* what
    is real.

Shibli loves soul and spirit.
Mevlana Rumi loves what is real.

Last night, I was calling to mind my friends,
one at a time, the depth of understanding in each, what
    they need.

So-and-so comes up. Why should he be like that? I ask.
I feel sorry for him. He is clearly one of us. He is.

That's why you are so delighted in your heart,
because you belong with us.

This is the way I do. *Inwardly,* I see the core
of a person's nature, the deep value.
Then I welcome him here, openly, *outwardly.*

I have said this a thousand times.
When I love someone, I act harshly,
unjustly so. For one small slipup
I respond a thousandfold.

Whereas with others that I have no connection with,
I ignore mountains of bad behavior.

When someone finds himself alone in a desert,
that's because of some estrangement from friends.

I am kind with such a one. I become his servant,
so far away he is from those he loves, so lost.

Have you noticed how solicitous I become with someone
who is not worthy to carry your old, wornout shoes?

I let his unconscious life go by without comment.

Remember. The saints and prophets were given
such difficulties to live through
because they were so deeply loved.

 53.

The difference between myself and the great beings
   is that
with me there is no distinction between inner and
   outer.

I can sit and talk with strangers,
or I can be with friends, even better.

When someone finds a particular path,
he goes deeply into it for a time.

Maybe then he gets confused.
He goes back and starts over.

Try to be consistent in your friendships.
Don't imagine foolish things about a friend.

Abu Bakr Rubabi has heard a lot about Nasruddin.
One day their paths cross, but no one
introduces them. They do not recognize each other.

Together, they rob a man who's coming along,
taking his donkey, his clothing, whatever he's carrying.

Crying, the guy hangs a little drum
around his neck and beats it,
saying, *I hope they don't steal my naked body too.*
They steal the drum.

These friendly rogues become competitive
about their thievery. One shows some new skill.
The other tops it. Finally Abu Bakr:
Who are you, with all this wit and trickery?

Nasruddin.

So that's it. It's all true then, what I've heard.

Like that, two dervishes,
deep heart-knowers, meet.

One bows and is very reverential toward the other.
That is his way, kindness and being polite.

The other knows that the first is following
an *accustomed* way, so he acts rudely.

He knows that the deepest happiness, the truest peace,
comes when one learns to deal with cruelty.

He himself knows well
that way into felicity,

so he gives it to his friend, this knowing that he knows
more clearly than he does even the disk
of the sun in the sky each day.

 54.

A fierce clarity looks at gentleness
and sees only itself, harshness, severity.

If I call you an *unbeliever,*
I mean that you and I both exist within God,
but that I am, at the moment, the quality of kindness
and you are the quality of harsh judgment.

Mercy always takes precedence.
Move beyond the judging.
Merge with gentleness. It tastes better.

In other words, whatever is here
is meant to be.

With some qualities, though, the radiance
is covered. Then the veil becomes
a spell that *lifts* the veil!

The inner meaning that all the prophets
and all sacred books are saying
is this: *Find a mirror.*
A way to see *yourself,* as an other.

55.

Before Ibrahim left his kingdom,
the city of Balkh, he became aware
that nothing was working for him.

Not the many ascetic acts, not the wealth
that he had spent on his desires, on all that he wanted.

He kept saying to himself, Still no opening comes,
no opening. What further should I do?

One night he was sleeping on the throne,
napping, awake, then sleeping again.

The palace guards on patrol outside were calling out,
beating their sticks together. While Ibrahim wondered
within himself, Which enemy are they keeping away?

The real enemy is here, sleeping and waking
    within me.
I need God's grace, not these noisy nightwatchmen!
The true security is inside that gentleness.

These thoughts are for Ibrahim
a kind of dozing madness.

Then, he hears footsteps on the roof above him.
A loud coming and going overhead.
Where are those guards now?
Don't they see this crowd on the palace roof?

A panic comes. He cannot move or call out.
A man looks down from the roof and says quietly,
So who are *you,* sitting on that throne?

I am the king. Who are you?

We have lost two, or maybe it's three, strings of camels.
We are looking for those here on the palace roof.

Ibrahim says, Are you mad?

The man on the roof replies, You are the one
    who's mad!

Do you think it's normal to look for lost camels
    up there?

The man: Yet you consider it sane to look for God
on the throne of a kingdom? Is *that* where you expect
to find such a vast, unnameable, inner and outer grace?

That was it for Ibrahim.
He saw the absurdity of his life, suddenly.

Gone. He went, and no one
after that could find him anywhere.

 56.
There are many things I don't say.
I say about a third of what I know.

People insist on describing someone as "all gentleness,"
and it's true. A certain man may be a complete
    kindness.
But then they imagine that is perfection. It is not.

God is not *all* gentleness.
There must be both harshness, a severe clarity, *and*
    kindness.
Without both, you are just whimsical, imaginary,
and stupid. Shallow, capricious.

Someone proposes a corollary: Be severe with your
    enemies

and kind toward friends. But not everyone can
  recognize
who is a friend and who is an enemy. Remember
  the poem:

> *For you to distinguish between enemy and friend,*
> *you'll have to live your life over again.*

This is being said to one who has not died
to his first existence and woken into new life.

One who lives into the second life
sees within a new light, where he can recognize his
  friends
and also those who mean him harm.

Kindness when appropriate, *soul fury* in its place.
But really, they both go back to the same source.

 57.

When you long for a blessing,
you are longing for more, more life,
more of whatever you have already been given,

and this is good, very good, this excess.
Want more than being a dervish.

Want more than being a Sufi or a mystic.
MORE! More of each stage that you come into.
Let your longing keep you in motion. In your
    prayers
when you say *Allahu Akbar,* God is Great,
you mean that God is great-*er* than anything
you might imagine. Great-er than all concepts
and all your experience. When you want more,
you are acknowledging how God is always *more.*

 58.

I left so that you could mature in your soul.
Separation cooks the seeker.

I would like it more if you could do this cooking
without my going away. I have no right
to tell you to go on a journey somewhere,
so I must do the going-away, for your sake.

With distance, you see your own station better.
You realize that the difficulties of being together
were nothing compared to those of separation.

I would go away fifty times if that would help.
It makes absolutely no difference to me where I am.
Istanbul, Syria, anywhere throughout Anatolia, the
    Kaaba.

All that matters is your work. All that matters is
how my being apart from you can perfect your spirit.

 59.

What *frees* you is not words, but rather someone's
    presence,
their actual being. *That* is the scripture you must
    attend to.

The power that I am hoping to give
does not come into you by following a line of words
across a page. A real lineage comes down
through personal interaction with others.

60.

Shams could not stand people who get their awareness from books and not direct experience. Whenever he heard a scholastic theologian talking, he felt compelled to confront him. Here is an exchange he had with one who was expounding on the text, *And He is with you wherever you are* (Qur'an 57:5).

But what exactly does that *mean*? Tell us, how is God with *you*?

> And what exactly do you *mean* by asking me that
> question?
> He was about to explode with anger.

You have this annoying habit of not saying what you mean.
How is God with you?

> In my knowing.

But knowledge is not separate from essence.
No quality is apart from essence.

> You are asking stale, old questions.

What do you mean, *old*? These are new,
absolutely fresh matters.

So this is how scholars act nowadays?

 61.

Rumi has become so innocent in his knowledge.
He's like that little Russian boy
that we see on the street here in Konya now
with a cone-shaped hat, selling matches.
He has no ego left; he's gone.

Don't tell Rumi this, but he himself is in exactly the
    right place
for being either a master or a disciple.

Empty, surrendered. Many are in such a place.
But there is a way that goes beyond this.

 62.

I have never acted like a master with Rumi.
I came here with the understanding that I would *not*

be his teacher. No one has yet lived
who could be that!

And I can no longer be anyone's student.
That is no longer in me.

I came here for the refuge of friendship.
For someone with whom I can be true to myself,
no hypocrisy, no pretending anything.

Most of the great teachers have been hypocrites.
They have gone against their own heart's truth.

 63.

We need to be clear from the first
how this is going to go. Friendship and brotherhood,
or teacher and pupil? Not that last.
I have no interest in that.

 64.

Real growing does not come from books,
but rather from walking out and doing things!

65.

People come to me with their problems.
I give them fresh answers, ten for every question!

Gracefully put, clear, and never found
in any book. Rumi once said, Since I have known you,
these books I have been so fond of
read like dead text.

66.

Rumi gets lost in the ecstasy of his kindness,
but he loses his clarity within that.
He surrenders to that state and forgets everything.

Whereas I retain control of my awareness.
I feel the same loving awareness,
but I don't get lost in the love-ecstasy as he does.

67.

Such blessing! I am so fortunate to be here
seeing your face. Now, anyone who wants to *see*
the Prophet should come here and look at your face

when you're completely relaxed,
not giving a discourse or conducting a ceremony.

Who am I that I should get to know Rumi
in this way? I'll tell you. Someone *very* happy.

 68.

I have a good mind, and I speak with some eloquence,
but I was just water boiling in a pot,
turning over on myself, within myself.

Then inside Rumi's presence I began to flow out
from that container. What I am now
feels like a spring, clear, constantly new,
and more helpful to the community.
Such pleasure this is!

 69.

What does pre-eternity mean to you? What is your
    origin?
The source? What is spirit?

Spend your life finding out your own state.
Those other mysteries will come clear.

God is depth. And you, you fool, you are also deep.
That same depth is in *you*.

Don't worry about terminology, *pre-existence,*
the original face, spirit, soul.
Search within yourself. The great mystery is there.
Everyone talks about *gnosticism* and *dervishes.*
Those are just words.

I want someone with a pulse, a living friend,
who says directly to me, *You are a part. I am the whole.*
Come into this awareness. Get to know me.

 70.

I have been sent here to take you away
from these coarse people who are wasting your time.

Sixteen years ago I heard you speaking. We met.
I said my salaams, but you did not respond. You left.

I was strongly drawn to you, but I saw revealed
in your way of speaking then that you were not ready
for the secret I carry. Even if I had told you then,
it would not have been right. We would not have had
the moment that we have now, in this present time.

Your soul was not in the state where you are now.

 71.

Of all the divine mysteries, we have been given only
  an *alif,*
a single stroke down.

Everything else is meant to explain that one stroke.
We talk about what's written on the tablet, on the earth,
on the heart, but tell me about that *alif,*
and I'll explain the rest of the alphabet.

The intellect is so weak and inept.
What's most real is in that *alif,*
which we do not yet understand.

72.

A mirror has no prejudgment.
You can beg it not to reveal some blemish on your
    friend's face,
"Please, it's a small flaw. You will hurt his feelings."

But the state of the mirror is such that it *must* answer,
"I'm sorry. That's impossible.
I have to reveal what comes before me."

If your friend cannot stand to see his own faults,
try not to give him the mirror, or tell him
that there's something wrong with the reflecting
    surface,
but that's even worse.

Author's Note on Translation

These short free-verse poems are versions of Rumi's *rubai,* done from Gamard and Farhadi's translations. Making versions is a way, I feel, of entering, and praising, and bringing Rumi's insights into my own life. I can best do that, it seems, by putting scholarly translations into my own short-poem tradition, which is a constantly moving composite of many lineages. I love the beauty of translated short poems from many cultures: Roman (Catullus), Greek (fragments of Heraclitus), Anglo-Saxon and Welsh (the medieval riddles, elegies, and other short poems), Japanese haiku (Bashō, Buson, Issa), Chinese (Li Po, Tu Fu, Po Chu'i), English (Shakespeare, Wyatt, Keats, Donne), Irish (Hopkins, Yeats, Kavanagh), Kabir and Tagore from India, the Cree Indian poems (Howard Norman's work). I love the American poets too (Emily Dickinson, William Carlos Williams, Stafford, Bly, Galway Kinnell, Mary Oliver, and many others). I am trying to create a new aesthetic for the here and now of how we are.

Making versions is a form of interpretation and, hopefully, a way of transmission, despite what Shams says about the ineffectiveness of the printed word (#59). I have been about this practice since 1976. Several books have come out of it: *The Essential Rumi, The Book of Love, The Big Red Book.* Ibrahim Gamard, Rawan Farhadi, William Chittick, and Franklin Lewis disapprove of making versions. I understand the objection. What I do is a homemade, amateurish, loose, many-stranded thing, without much attention to historical context, nor much literal faithfulness to the original. I did not hear Rumi's name until I was thirty-nine.

I claim only to be a poet in American English. I leave the judgment of how well that has gone to others. I also leave the judgment to others as to how deeply I understand the spiritual mysteries coming through Rumi's poetry. I will never know, I guess, how much I miss, how much is coming through that is valid transmission, how much distortion. It could be said that all translation is distortion, to varying degrees. How could one possibly translate Shakespeare into Chinese? For example:

> I know you all, and will awhile uphold
> the unyoked humor of my idleness,
> yet herein will I imitate the sun,
> who doth permit the base contagious clouds
> to smother up his beauty from the world.
> *(Henry IV, Part 1)*

That music. I have no idea how it could be done, but many have tried, as well they should, and should continue to. They must.

So how to translate Rumi into American free verse? It may be, as the French say, that translation is always a betrayal of the original poem. *Traduir, c'est trahir.* To translate is to betray. I try to hear what's coming through Rumi's poems and Shams' *Sayings,* and to translate that through my own understanding, my own energy, staying true to their images. It's all about a kind of vitality coming through the language. I try to make a new poem in American English. When a non-Persian-speaking English-language speaker (which is what I am) reads a literal translation of a Rumi poem, along with the notes and commentary, he must then make up a poem in his mind that is not on the page. I try to put something down *on the page* that has a life of its own somewhat akin to the vital presence of Rumi's words. It's all mystical, imaginary work, and of course it's impossible. I have only my *sensing* through the more literal translation of what the poem *might* be. But it has been my practice and my delight, my folly, for almost forty years now.

When I first began, in 1976, I was teaching three college English classes a day. After finishing, in the late afternoon, I would go down to the Bluebird Cafe in Athens, Georgia, and sit there with some hot tea, and work on a single Arberry* Rumi poem for an hour or so. It was not *work* at all. It was, and continues to be, a sublime kind of play and relaxation. A deep relief from the explicating of poems involved in teaching literature. It took me out of my mind into a place where mind does not work so well. Heart and some other center of being are more active there. You can walk around and breathe in a new place. It's a kind of trance that I go into there in the Bluebird Cafe, or in Jittery Joe's Coffeehouse, or home sitting before a fire, or in the cabin beside Fightingtown Creek—the places I go to let these collaborations occur.

I would not have much sense of what it might have been like in Rumi's community if I had not sat in Bawa Muhaiyaddeen's room and heard him sing spontaneous songs and answer questions. Visiting Osho's commune in Poona, when he was still there, was also good. Robert Bly and Galway Kinnell have been companions, in dream and out. Lisa Starr and her animals. In one of his quatrains, Rumi says, "Tonight we are here with a thousand hidden mystics." I don't make any extravagant claims (well, maybe a few), but I do feel sometimes that there are helping presences. Bawa once told me that he knew Rumi and Shams Tabriz not like people in a book but, he said, "I know them like I know you." Of course, as I work on these poems, I don't have the Persian to consult. I literally have nothing to be faithful to, except what the scholars give. Mostly, I like the way I have spent these years. At seventy-seven, this is probably the last volume. Maybe not. I still delight

---

* The Cambridge Islamicist A. J. Arberry has two important collections of Rumi ghazals: *Mystical Poems of Rumi* (Chicago and London: University of Chicago Press, 1968) and *Mystical Poems of Rumi,* second selection (Boulder, CO: Westview Press, 1979).

in stumbling about in the *Masnavi*. The work has brought me wonderful friends. I am very grateful. May those two astonishing human God-beings, Rumi and Shams Tabriz, be blessed in the grandeur of their friendship.

Then there's the matter of my commentaries and the notes. I allow myself lots of leeway in those, much variation in tone. Bits of personal life slip in. I once told James Hillman, when I sent him a book, "Begin with the notes." It was *The Drowned Book: Ecstatic and Earthy Reflections by Bahauddin, the Father of Rumi* (2004). He was kind. "I did finally read the commentary in *The Drowned Book* that you suggested (imposed on my Jewish obligatory conscience to read) and was overjoyed, really and truly, happy with it, from it. You've got a freedom of phrase or rhythm or an access to a little pile of Georgia kindling wood that is lightweight and touches off big logs burning. Lucky man. Let me know when you get North and East. We have not danced together for ten years!" We all miss James' dance.

Notes on the Rumi Quatrains

The first number below refers to my numbering of the quatrains, 1–217. For instance, #2 refers to my version with that number. The second number, No. 1787, refers to its place in the complete translation of Rumi's quatrains, *The Quatrains of Rumi,* by Ibrahim W. Gamard and A. G. Rawan Farhadi (San Rafael, CA: Sufi Dari Books, 2008). Their numbering goes from 1 to 1959. Their scholarship is magnificent, comprehensive, and deeply intuitive. We are greatly indebted to them. Anyone who loves Rumi and Shams should own a copy.

#2—No. 1787—I once asked Bawa Muhaiyaddeen* if what I saw in his eyes could ever come up behind my eyes and look out. He often answered my questions with a pun. "When the eye (I) becomes a we." He was speaking of the dissolving of the ego, when a singular self becomes plural, or nothing at all. Surely that is what an *elder* is: someone who has left self-absorption behind, whose being has become the community, or the emptiness around it.

---

* Bawa was a teacher of mine, a Sri Lankan Sufi who became a more universal teacher. He came to me in a dream on May 2, 1977. I met him in this visible world a year and a half later. I visited him four or five times a year for nine years, until his death on December 8, 1986. My connection to him has been very important in the effort to have a living relationship with Rumi's poetry. I have told the story of that meeting, in detail, in several places: *The Essential Rumi,* expanded edition, pp. 363–65; *Rumi: The Book of Love,* pp. 140–41; *The Soul of Rumi,* pp. xv–xvii; and *Rumi: The Big Red Book,* pp. 160–61 (all published by HarperOne).

#3—No. 1449—This wonderful poem was almost lost. Gamard and Farhadi say that it survives in only one of Furuzanfar's manuscripts. Most *rubai* appear in several.

#6—No. 1461—One of the Ninety-Nine Beautiful Names is the Gatherer, *Jami.* Others might be Scatterer, Stayer at Home, and Mother.

#9—No. 1177—One expects the great mystics to recommend silence, but here Rumi says to *be always talking more, more!* Volubility. He comes back often to this metaphor of the swift-running stream. See #20, #46, and #74. It reminds me of Lao Tze and his *watercourse way.* The Tao.

#12—No. 1266—Wandering the city at night is heart-intelligence, contrasted here with mind-intellect, which likes to make sense and *put things in context,* and is not so interested in wandering the night. My friend John Seawright used to be a devotee of walking the streets at night, but it is not just a young man's restless way. I see old men out walking too. It's an opening.

#13—No. 1893—Bahauddin, Rumi's father, speaks this poem after saying that the human body is given some release in sleep and that there our consciousness comes to know other dimensions besides this physical one (*The Drowned Book,* p. 57).

In the second stanza, the changeover into fall has always seemed, to me, the most creative, the most full of soul-potential of all the seasonal transitions. That first cool, windy October day in Georgia.

#14—No. 1817—Shams was called *Parinda, bird, the one who flies away.* It is said that whenever people gathered around him to be taught, he would find some excuse to leave the group, and then disappear. Gone, left town. It is also said that he would never accept pay for his work. He was a mason. When he got paid, he would find a way to put the money in someone else's coat.

#15—No. 1951—This is attributed to Baba Afzaluddin (d. 1274), but Gamard and Farhadi are fairly sure that the first two lines of the second stanza are Rumi's.

#16—No. 1834—This poem may be read as a gloss on Qur'an 50:16: "We [Allah] created man. We know the promptings of his soul, and are closer to him than his jugular vein" (Dawood translation). Many of Rumi's poems are glosses on, or unfoldings of, Qur'anic passages.

#17—No. 1835—Nonexistence is another name for the mystery that he sometimes calls *the friend* or *the beloved*. Shams Tabriz and sunlight. Shams, in Arabic, means "the sun."

A distinction is made here between being "in love" and being "in nonexistence." In oneness (nonexistence), there are not "many different lives." No lover, no beloved. I do not claim to understand this very well. But please don't try to help me with it. I would rather talk about what was walking on my roof last night. Most likely the big raccoon, scary as death, that I saw coming toward me down the driveway, like my wild cousin Tom Lamar. I may be beginning to understand nonexistence. Every word that Rumi spoke comes from there.

#18—No. 1842—"Here I am" is what pilgrims say as they move around the Kaaba. You have come all this way. For what? *For you.*

#19—No. 1837—"Shut up," Lisa Starr and I have decided, means, "I love you."

#21—No. 1347—More images of the grieving emptiness. The cage, "released of its bird," and the birdsong of the flown one, which has a fragrance of "eternity in tears."

#22—No. 1883—This is a Kermani (d. 1238) quatrain. All such textual information, of course, comes from Gamard and Farhadi's text. This one from p. 589. Rumi evidently made small changes in Kermani's poem and put it in his own collection. In the thirteenth century, poets were not as concerned as we are about copyright and intellectual ownership. They would not have accepted such claims. We are all in this together, they say instead, trying to sing praise and make beauty. They celebrate a communal creativity. It's a chorus. Find a poem you love by anybody, change it to suit you, and include it in "your" collection. To our jealous and competitive minds here in the twenty-first century, their fluidity seems like petty theft. It's hard to imagine what *a book* was in the thirteenth century. It must have felt like a rare, invaluable complex of overlapping worlds, something as gorgeously alive as a city in central Asia. Balkh, Chigil, Samarkand.

Rumi may have gotten inspiration from this Kermani poem for the opening of the *Masnavi,* the famous image there about the crying sound of the reed flute and how its music makes everyone weep in empathy for their own separation from the reedbed-union, that experience of nearness and silence, the sugar-making of having no ego.

I am seeing more and more how much grief work is in these poems. The emptiness that comes through the reed flute's music is helpful to others because it lets them grieve openly. *Lacrimae rerum,* the tears of things, as Virgil says.

#28—No. 597—How does a friend live in a friend? Bawa Muhaiyaddeen used to call those who came to his room, anyone, *the lightpoints in my eyes.* I'm not sure that I know what that means, though I feel it about my children and grandchildren sometimes.

#31—No. 897—This poem may be a gloss on Qur'an 82:8, "Into whatever shape He willed, He could have moulded you."

#34—No. 902—It is impossible to put into English Rumi's elegant pun in the Persian. *Parwana* in Persian means "moth" and, astonishingly, "an official letter." In the punning play of this poem, the moth is an official letter saying, *I am yours.* A letter comes; it's from the king!

#35—No. 1406—This poem is in the mood of Sufis on the path of blame, the *malamatiya.* Humility is their way. They take the blame for everything. No spiritual pride at all. It is not a pose. They mean it, very deeply. Gamard and Farhadi tell us that "we are rubbing" is *mal-em,* and "blame" is *malam,* so with the wordplay we might consider ourselves *malamatiya,* blame-rubbing (dregs on our faces) confessors of guilt. I am told that those on the path of blame have no interior pretension and no exterior affectations. The secret of their friendship with the divine is that sometimes it is not apparent *to them.* They remain hidden, to themselves and to others. They practice a deep sincerity and honesty. They feel that most decadence in soul-life comes from wishing to preserve one's "good name" and "reputation." Such things must be disregarded.

#38—No. 1830—The image of the cave with a market square at the end of it is intriguing. I have always been drawn to caves, growing up as I did in the limestone country of eastern Tennessee, which is riddled with amazing caves, sacred territory for me. Then in the 1990s I was lucky enough to go into the Les Trois Frères cave in southern France, all the way back to where the sorcerer dances fifteen feet above a swarm of animals. So the image here implies that at the inward end of what we do (our craft) and what we are (the friend), there is a vital community exchanging goods and ideas and laughter.

The *hidden* line is an echo of the famous hadith where God explains why the universe exists: *I was a hidden treasure and I wanted to be known.*

#45—No. 1073—The joy of the soul is in the opening of laughter.

#55—No. 693—Salamanders, say the alchemists, love to live inside fire.

#56—No. 1708—*Khor-khor* is Persian for "snore." Poets very rarely put actual snoring in a poem.

#58—No. 1740—My mother used to say, in amused outrage at some foolishness, "Ye gods and little fishes," from her ocean-heart.

Rumi advises that we should gamble away our wealth, but what exactly is that *wealth*? What we think of as our own? What is the ocean? The limitless let-go of living in the heart?

Sometimes I can spontaneously let language come and go. I said *Salaam aleichem* to a wonderfully garrulous group of Muslim men just out of Friday night prayers, gathered in an Athens, Georgia, coffeehouse. Mostly they were from Amman, Jordan, but from all over the Near East too—Beirut, Cairo, Tunis, Damascus.

They turned and smiled. "Aleichem salaam, my brother."

All of us then were der-fish, let out of school.

#59—No. 1261—This tavern comes up again and again in Rumi's poetry, as the ecstatic place we all were in before this existence, not just Muslims and Christians and Jews, but Jains and Hindus, Native Americans, Mayans, Incas, Aztecs, Bushmen, all indigenous cultures, Buddhists, the members of all the religions on this amazing blue planet. (Those in other galaxies too, if any there be.) Also in that tavern were the millions with no official religion, who are agnostic, or willing to wait and see, or not interested in defining such things. They may be aware of numinous moments, and they are willing to wait for more. Also, the love religion folks, who have no sanctuary and no belief system, just a rose above the door. That's the way the Sufis invite the mystics of every lineage to meet with them. No one is denied entry to this tavern. No one checks IDs at this door.

Rumi sometimes calls it the *Am I Not (Yes!)* tavern because of the covenant of Alast (mentioned in Qur'an 7:172—not the tavern but the covenant). There was a moment (!) in pre-eternity when Allah asked us formless ones, *Am I not your Lord?* We all answered YES! so quickly that the answer was simultaneous with the question. So it takes two to say the tavern's name. Better a whole crowd, a flashmob playing Beethoven's "Ode to Joy." The covenant of Alast is mentioned in Qur'an 7:172, but the *Yes!* is not there. Instead, in Dawood, the more serene answer, "We bear witness that you are."

#62—No. 1084—A definite appetite for fish and bread, new promptings, new things to love (like Paul Auster's *Winter Journal,* today) arrive from the same generous, infinitely inventive source.

#63—No. 1368—Getting released to the sky is one of the oldest human longings and satisfactions. Pre-Columbian shell gorgets have been found on Williams Island in the Tennessee River that have carved on them men with wings, dancing, imagining flight or actually, shamanically, doing it. My childhood bedroom window looked out across that island. There is evidence that people have lived there for 15,000 years.

#67—No. 1718—*Qutb* is a fairly esoteric Sufi term. *Pole* might be better. *Axis, center.* Rumi is said to be the Pole of Love; Gilani, the Pole of Power; Ibn Arabi, the Pole of Intellect. *Qutb* means "axis," a *center* that contains the periphery or is present in it. The *qutb* is a spiritual being, or a function, that can reside in a human being or several human beings, a movement or a moment. It is the elusive mystery of how the divine gets delegated into the manifest world. It can never be defined. Bawa once said, laughing, that Rumi was the *qutb*. Maybe the friendship of Rumi and Shams was/is the *qutb*. Or say their friendship is one of the many blessings on this majestically turning planet.

#72—No. 440—There is a subtle wordplay here in Persian that cannot be duplicated in English. Gamard and Farhadi tell us that the word for "form" and "appearance" can also mean "face," so that hidden in every line of the poem is the irresistible answer. I put the answer in a last line, but if I understand the scholars correctly, the answer does not appear in the poem in Farsi. It is just always there, concealed as nuance, in the language. Nor does the word *riddle* appear in the original. It is implied.

#74—No. 1579—Carl Jung calls this "cosmogonic love." He says, "For we are in the deepest sense the victims and the instruments of cosmogonic 'love.' I put the word in quotation marks to indicate that I do not use it in its connotations of desiring, preferring, favoring, wishing, and similar feelings, but as something superior to the individual, a unified and undivided whole."

#75—No. 1464—What is the one subject that Shams will not talk about? Perhaps the dangerous truth discussed in the introduction to the Shams section. But more likely, it is that subject which all the mystics speak of, that which is unnameable, so close that we cannot say, that we walk around inside. . . .

#79—No. 1375—Rumi at the end of this sounds like Shams in excerpt #40 from his *Sayings:* "The difficulty that I have with living has to do with my not being this or that, or that or this, or *anything.*"

#82—No. 553—This *you,* this aliveness, is what makes inner and outer one beingness.

#87—No. 635—I added the word *grandeur* here. I once had a dream in which I was being warned against not honoring the "grandeur of Rumi's surrender." I try to heed such warnings.

#88—No. 650—This is a conversation with Shams Tabriz, as are many of Rumi's poems. Shams is dismissive here, contemptuous even, of the impulse to write anything down. Gamard and Farhadi tell us that in Persian the word for "verse" can also mean "house." Shams says words cannot contain anything that is as real as he is.

#89—No. 659—One can get too preoccupied with dreams. I surely have, with my archive of 130 dream journals. Rumi says here that there needs to come a whole-cloth change to night itself, or to what night means in human consciousness.

#98—No. 1147—The lines at the end are quoting Qur'an 21:104. This entire poem in in Arabic.

#104—From a note on No. 1902, Gamard and Farhadi, p. 594, saying that Rumi spoke this to his students, though not in the form of a poem. He is again addressing the mystery of human identity. He says that who he is, is not a person occurring in history or someone who can be known through reading his poetry, but a certain taste inside *you*. Bawa Muhaiyaddeen used to talk about the *taste* of what he knew. In the preface to Book II of the *Masnavi*, Rumi quotes the Arab saying, *He who does not taste, does not know.*

#106—No. 1848—Why do we thwart ourselves? Why not accept the great joy that is given us? This is a facetious question on my part. I know well enough why I hesitate to surrender. Ego. The habitual familiarity of staying with the limits within which I am comfortable—and stuck.

#108—No. 1580—Many of Rumi's poems are about this "something different," a love, a friendship that is finding new forms, new words, new ways to use the old pronouns. It cannot be expressed, but we must try.

#111—No. 1456—Of this version of Khidr-love, nothing can be said. There is a flow inside it, carrying us along, the Tao that can be tasted, felt, but not spoken.

#112—No. 1458—Someone specific is being addressed at the end of this poem, someone evidently not in resonance with Rumi's ecstatic joy.

#115—No. 1840—This is a gloss on Qur'an 84:19, "You will travel from stage to stage," combined with Qur'an 5:115–17, where Jesus prays for a table spread with food.

#117—No. 1912—There is a wonderful passage in Aflaki* where Shams challenges some religious scholars for their lack of genuine inspiration. He quotes this anonymous poem to show them what the real thing sounds like, and then has this to say: "We do not know who he was, the person who spoke this poem. He may have had no real knowledge of the condition it reveals. He may be an illiterate farmer. Nevertheless, Sanai, Nizami, Kharraqani, and Attar speak *through* him in this quatrain. With all their soul-experience they are collaborating with this simple villager." When Shams says this to the scholars, Rumi, in a state of sudden ecstatic knowledge, stands up and *dives* into the pool there. He says nothing. Robes still on, he dives, in an act of pure astonishment.

#123—No. 1107—Shirts are so important in the Joseph story. Smelling Joseph's shirt restores Jacob's sight. Joseph's shirt, torn from behind,

---

* Aflaki, *The Feats of the Knowers of God,* trans. John O'Kane (Leiden: Brill Publishers, 2002), 447–48.

proves his innocence with Zuleikha. Then there is Joseph's amazing technicolor dreamcoat.

#127—No. 1248—The American poet Hayden Carruth says that *heart* is a "genteel and banal word." I almost agree, but I cannot always find ways to avoid it.

#128—No. 1672—Rumi does not mention the Kunduz Valley in northern Afghanistan, but he might well have tasted, as a boy in nearby Balkh, those multicolored jewelboxes. I heard about their legendary variety of color and taste from an Afghan taxi driver in Minneapolis. I love how Rumi finds an image for the coming of soul-blessings in *melons.*

#129—No. 1859—This poem is by Hakim Sanai.

#130—No. 1870—Rumi's son, Sultan Velad, quotes this Attar quatrain in his *Maarif* to illustrate the following passage: "How can the mystery be hidden when the divine qualities are innumerable and creation is infinite? As the Qur'an says, *Whichever way you turn, there is the Face of God* (Qur'an 2:115). That mystery is more present, more evident, than existence itself. There can be no proof for something so obvious."

#132—No. 833—An intense jet black is mentioned in Qur'an 35:27. Gamard and Farhadi think the creative crow feather here may refer to that.

Rumi often associates the lifting of the heart in spring with laughter, sprouting. Fire catches, water pours, wind rises. And the crows. They talk to me, no matter the season, every time I go outdoors.

#138—No. 123—Shams calls this horse *soul fury*. Rumi refers to it in #65 as the *horse of great longing*.

#142—No. 1738—I am told that *Mevlana* (Rumi) comes from the same stem as *reveille*. The one awake in all his parts is whole. He is recommending here that we wake into a consciousness (a companion to walk with) where all is integrated into one.

#146—No. 1281—Gamard and Farhadi suggest that the black thread may be a reference to Qur'an 2:187.

#148—No. 1549—*You* and the wine of *this*. He says elsewhere, *There is no need to look anywhere for this one, who is your whole life.* "The Friend," in *The Big Red Book,* p. 225.

#149—This poem is by Rumi's son, Sultan Velad, found in his *Divan* #335.

#150—Another by Sultan Velad, *Divan* #346.

#152—No. 1878—A quatrain by Sayfuddin Bakharzi (d. 1232). It is included in a Kermani collection. The editor there says that it should be thought of as a Rumi quatrain, though probably written by Bakharzi (?!). See Gamard and Farhadi, p. 588. These are called *floating quatrains,* because they move from collection to collection with small changes. They seem to me to indicate that these poets knew a truth we are sometimes skeptical of: human beings are not discrete. In our creativity, especially, we work collectively. In tandem, in threes and fours, by the tableful, by the continent.

#153—No. 434—Is this the mysterious source of spontaneity, the dear speaker inside, who keeps changing the part we play?

#155—No. 1754—Sleep is such a wash.

#159—No. 1766—To balance the sexist (thirteenth century) mindset present in the last two lines, one might rephrase them:

> When a mother tells her child a story,
> she does not think she is a child.

Or more awkwardly (to my ear):

> When a parent tells a child a story,
> he or she does not think she or he is a child.

Likewise, one might rephrase #6, the "Love is the mother" poem:

> Love, you are the father.
> All these are your children.

In the scholars' literal translations *father* is present in #159 and *mother* is there in #6. Perhaps a reader should feel free, as I have, to adapt these poems to the truth of one's own life, whenever the language allows.

#163—No. 1881—A story is told in Aflaki (pp. 84–85) and in Gamard and Farhadi (in the note to No. 1881, p. 589) about how this poem came to be. Rumi speaks it (or perhaps quotes a poem by Kermani) to settle a question of protocol, about who should sit where in the meeting room. The gathering is in the king's palace, by special invitation. All the local dignitaries are there—the great scholars, the recluses, the travelers come from other countries. When Rumi's group arrives, Husam Chelebi (Rumi's chief disciple) comes in first and goes to the raised dais. Other prominent men from the community join him, so that when Rumi enters, there is no place on the *soffa,* the extended seat where teachers sit. Rumi sits down on the floor. No problem. Husam immediately joins him there, as do some others from the dais. The proud, though, the hypocrites, stay in their exalted seats. A discussion begins. Many subtle minds are there; they pose the question: *In the present situation, where is the seat of honor?* One says, "In the middle of the raised platform, the traditional place for the teacher." Another, "But according to those who practice spiritual withdrawal, it is in the far corner of the lodge, the *zaviya*." Still another, "Among Sufis it is just there beside the platform where people remove their shoes." They turn to Rumi: "What is your opinion on this?" Rumi says, "Where is the doorway? Where is the most honored seat? Where are we, each one of us? Where am I? Wherever the friend is." "But where is the friend?" someone shouts. This is the big question in a Sufi community, the one you ask with your whole life. *The friend is your whole life.* Rumi speaks this poem, No. 1881, in answer to that question. Then he stands up and begins to turn. The *sema* becomes so heart-surrendered that many of the prominent citizens tear their expensive robes and keep on dancing, all pretension abandoned.

#164—No. 1879—The *name* mentioned here at the end might be Kermani, Razi, Abil Khayr, Baba Afzaluddin Kashi, or Rumi, according to Gamard and Farhadi (p. 588). Maybe all of them in collaboration. This may be the freest-floating of all free-floating quatrains.

#165—No. 1361—There seem to be two kinds of burning here. The burning of practicing patience, a discipline, which burns the clothes, the outer. Perhaps a repression? Then there's the burning of the voice, of passionate *expression,* which extends into spirit, into nonexistence.

#166—No. 1365—He is talking of his friendship with Shams Tabriz, how it brings the poetry *through* him into the world, and how at other times it clears and makes him empty, open, transparent. This is the secret of their friendship and its creativity. Both presences are needed for the unique vitality, the new consciousness, that they bring into being.

#167—No. 1925—This poem may be by Najmuddin Razi, or by his spiritual master Majduddin Baghdadi, or by Kermani, or even by Rumi.

#170—No. 1337—This poem feels, to me, like it comes from the tandem consciousness of Rumi/Shams. Rumi (and Shams) would claim that they all come from there, but this one so clearly does. You can feel the definite presence of soul fury.

#171—No. 909—The image of running out onto an open field is one that Rumi loves, the excitement every child has felt. I am reminded of a story from my own childhood. I am about four or five. I am lifted from my bath, dried off in a big towel. Then I bolt, down the front hall to the porch, out the screen door, running naked in the cool spring night. My brother Herb is chasing me, laughing, with our parents behind him. Through the tower, down four flights of three steps each, out onto the flat expanse of the quadrangle, and into the nightsky. We lived on a prep school campus. The memory is very clear, but it ends there. Evidently, I was snagged up and out of my running ecstasy, carried home, and put to bed, but I have no recollection of any of that.

#172—No. 911—This poem is in Arabic.

#179—No. 676—I put the *soul fury* and *kindness* in there. Gamard and Farhadi's phrase is "the wine and sugar from your lips."

#180—No. 1459—See the cave sleepers story, Qur'an 18:9–26.

#188—No. 1785—The French, with their wonderful gastronomical culture, have a word for the preboiling time of tiny bubbles rising. *Pétillance,* the just-barely tiny-bubble time that tells the cook the full boil is about to come.

#193—No. 1205—Here the mystery he explores is what perceives the longing from within the wholeness, the One.

#197—A reference to the story of Jesus saying, "Who touched me?" A crowd was pressing round him and his disciples. Peter says, "Lord, it could have been anyone." Jesus says, "Still, I felt someone's touch. The healing power went out of me." A woman then comes and falls at his feet. She had come to be healed, and she had been (Luke 8:45–46). Then she realized that she could not do that secretly, unnoticed. To really *be,* you must *be seen.* "Appear as you are," says Rumi.

#199—No. 1786—Rumi speaks this poem as part of Discourse #25. He is talking about a blind animal, a worm, a mole, who lives happily in the darkness under the earth with no need for eyes or ears, as being similar to people who live content with no longing for spirit. He goes on to say that God has made those two worlds, one awake and one not, because if ecstatic joy and its vision were granted to everyone, then no one would stay here! There evidently needs to be a vital tension between the two realities, of those awake and those still unconscious.

#203—No. 1838—The second stanza refers to the saying of God (hadith) reported by Muhammad, "I am not contained in heaven or earth, but rather in the hearts of those who love me. Look for me there." See Gamard and Farhadi (p. 670, note 171). The story about Muhammad's childhood is not in Rumi's quatrain, but it is implied. See Gamard and Farhadi (p. 575, note 4 to No. 1836).

Two angels in white came and took his heart
out of his body, washed it in a golden bowl of snow,
then put it back in, cleansed of the one small black speck.

#205—No. 1196—As I understand Gamard and Farhadi, the music of this totally untranslatable poem rhymes the four chief components of physical and psychic experience: (1) the mind, the brain, the head; (2) the body, the working of the limbs and the organs; (3) heart, the emotions, the impulse to let go, to surrender, that which recognizes beauty; and (4) the soul, here spoken of as a joy that dances among, flows around and through, all the other parts and finds resonance in the sound-structure that holds this vast, small poem together.

#208—No. 444—Rumi feels the strangeness here of being *in time*. *This* on one day, *that* on another. We each have a birth day; we have a death day. And there is the play, in time, of our several identities, the one that *appears* and the one that *is* (see #197). I am reminded of a pun that Bawa used, when I asked him what poetry is. He repeated *poetry* three times in his version of my Southern accent (po-etry, bo-etry, bo-tree) until it came out "bo tree." "Poetry is like the bo tree. It grows up, then it bends down and where it touches ground, it puts down more roots." He did not elaborate further about how that grounding might relate to poetry. He left that with me. Poetry longs upward from a ground, a moment, an experience, then it bows and touches what nourishes it— spirit, soul—puts down more roots, longs upward again, and goes on. Under the bo tree, of course, is where Gautama the Buddha came to his enlightenment. For five hundred years after his death, I am told, there were no statues made of Buddha. Instead, there was an image of the bo tree. His personal limits disappeared there, into the tree.

#210—No. 772—Poetry and music together help strengthen the con- nection between human beings, the telepathy, the knowing, which are other words for love and friendship. Poetry and music help us cry and laugh, enter new regions of awareness. Words reveal us and help us merge, overlap, hold on. Of course, everything that human beings do does that too, or can: prayer, meditation, conversation, singing, walking, cooking, playing the cello, the flute, the drum, the ukulele, dreaming and discussing dreams, fixing shoes, sweeping the steps, looking up words in the dictionary, playing tag, and eating apricot pie. The Sufis know this. They experiment with many techniques and possibilities in their learning communities. One practice is called deep listening, or *sema*.

#212—No. 120—I can identify with a lot in this poem. I too loved to go to school and listen to the teacher, all the way through graduate school. My nickname in college was Cloudy. But I do not claim to have achieved the last stage, which he describes as wind. Pure spirit? A divine vitality and freedom?

#214—No. 1716—I emailed my friend Allaudin Mathieu, musician, composer, writer, and mystic-lover, to ask for help with this poem. "Is it that every moment has sound, and that sound is the heart?" Allaudin: "Yes. Since sound is the bridge between the sacred silence of *this now* and the *always-as-sound* of the pots-and-pans world. Hazrat Inayat Khan, the master who brought Sufism to the West, says that 'creation is the music of God.' And that 'earthly sound is so concrete that it dims the music of the absolute.' As far as my own experience is concerned, I can tell you that there are times, not many, but there *are* times when, listening to music, my ears became attuned to the *Shabd,* the expanse beyond mindfulness" (from his book *Bridge of Waves,* p. 204, where he quotes Hazrat Inayat Khan's *Mysticism of Sound*).

The present moment, and friendship, as sound, *heart-sound*. Such a beautiful, fresh image/idea.

#215—No. 895—Good bumper sticker: FORGET MEMORY.

#216—No. 1363—We thought we were lost in the fog. No, it's the ocean of God. We're moving through that grace.

#217—No. 993—I feel this forgetfulness strongly in myself. I have been too content with making books of these "verbal imaginations," often neglecting what is more real about being alive.

All these words on paper, these books that we claim to fill with longing. It's better to offer up our lives as we are living them, the conversations, the friendships.

Notes on the Shams Excerpts

The writer Andrew Harvey asked me to have a conversation with him, for a class he was teaching by conference call with three hundred students listening! A first for me. The subject was to be some of these fragments from Shams' *Sayings* (*Maqalat*). It became apparent in the midst of our conversation that such discussion might well have been one way that Shams' words were used: as catalysts for *conversation* in the many dervish communities where they resided for most of the eight hundred years that they remained hidden away from general circulation. As Rumi says at the end of a ghazal, "Listening to Shams is a fine way of deepening into soul."*

#12—Shams gets "very bored with too much gentleness." A refreshing sentiment to me. When faced with a situation calling for conventional politeness and hospitality, I can imagine Shams saying, "It's best that I avoid these times and places. They very quickly make me bitter and mean."

#13—Shams feels that sometimes Rumi's "kindness" keeps him (Rumi) from action, from doing something that would be more compassionate than just gazing "with kind eyes."

#14—Is Shams telling us not to do what I and others are doing—*not* to share these words of his? Maybe. I would also claim that he is saying

---

* Barks, *Rumi: The Big Red Book* (San Francisco: HarperOne, 2010), 260.

that his *soul fury* cannot be transmitted by language. It must be gotten directly through being in a person's presence.

#25—Shams is so clear about having to destroy what makes a person quarrelsome or boring. The ego must be burned away.

#32—*Soul fury* appears here in Chittick's text, just this once as far as I have found. I have taken that phrase to be a key to Shams' core. In the other instances where I have used that phrase (#21, #24, #33, and #56), it does not appear in Chittick's text. I have added it because I feel it is implied, and that it clarifies what Shams is saying. Actually, it seems to me that all of Shams' words come from that mystery, his *soul fury*.

#35—This feels like the most profound of all Shams' insights. It keeps on resonating.

#36—Great practical wisdom here, about having to say a poem out loud to really know what is being said. It needs to resonate through the body. Shams puts great emphasis on how the body knows and feels its knowing.

#40—The undefinable emptiness described here is at the core of his *soul fury*. I feel it is a different emptiness from what Rumi explores with the reed-flute imagery.

#53—Nasruddin and Juhi. Juhi is the name that Shams uses. Nasruddin, with his trickster wisdom, is the more familiar name to us.

#59—When Sufis talk about a *silsila*, a lineage, they mean the soul-essence that comes down through personal contact, not so much through books. Shams is speaking here of a freedom, a *soul fury* (and a kindness) that is transmitted in the meeting of embodied souls.

#61—The "way that goes beyond this" is what Shams is leading us toward. It has been said of one of Shams' early teachers, Sallebaf, that he understood the drunkenness of God but not the sobriety that comes after. Shams urges us into areas of the psyche for which we have no names.

#68—Shams describes the state of his being before his friendship with Rumi as a *boiling* in place. Then in Rumi's presence he becomes a *flow,* something in motion, like a spring, a stream that can give life to a community, less confined, more at ease with himself in motion, playful, contradictory. Here is a fine sense of how it felt to be in Rumi's company. There's a cooling, a flowing out from wherever you've been unnecessarily stuck. To be with these two is to know a new freedom of spirit.

#71—There is an echo here of Shams' first words to Rumi: "How is it that Muhammad said, 'We have not known You as we should have?'" The *alif* is just the beginning, the first stroke down of the Oneness, and we don't even understand that first stroke yet.

References for the Rumi Quatrains

I want to recommend and celebrate the magnificent scholarship of Ibrahim Gamard and Rawan Farhadi, whose texts I have used to produce these versions. They are amazingly thorough and deeply devotional.*

The first number below refers to my numbering of the quatrains, 1–217. The second (No. 1366, No. 1790, etc.) refers to where the translation from which I made my version appears in *The Quatrains of Rumi*. Their numbering goes from 1 to 1959. The F number is to the standard Furuzanfar edition in Persian.

#1—No. 1366; F-310. As long as I am alive . . .

#2—No. 1790; F-808. Find your place . . .

#3—No. 1449; F-1180. I am grumpy . . .

#4—No. 1568; F-401. Out of kindness comes . . .

#5—No. 769; F-1887. Every day at dawn . . .

#6—No. 1461; F-728. Love, what sort of thing . . .

#7—No. 1299; F-1962. I wander through . . .

#8—No. 446; F-1429. Tonight we are here . . .

#9—No. 1177; F-996. My thirsty heart, . . .

#10—No. 441; F-200. Look how dust-grains . . .

#11—No. 442; F-1035. Last night, alone . . .

The Quatrains of Rumi, translated by Ibrahim W. Gamard and A. G. Rawan Farhadi (San Rafael, CA: Sufi Dari Books, 2008).

References for the Shams Excerpts

Most of the Shams references are to William Chittick's translation of Shams' *Maqalat, Me and Rumi: The Autobiography of Shams-i Tabrizi* (Louisville, KY: Fons Vitae, 2004). The first number refers to my numbering of the excerpts. The number with the # sign in front designates a section in the third part of his book, "My Time with Mawlana." The page number that follows is to that section. The number in parentheses refers to Mohammed-Ali Movahhed's edition of the Shams material in Persian, published in two volumes, in 1977 and 1990. Chittick includes those references to the Movahhed text. All the Chittick references are from the third section of his book, except #49, #50, and #71, which are from the second section, "My Path to God." Anyone interested in Rumi and Shams should have many of William Chittick's books close at hand: *The Sufi Path of Love: The Spiritual Teachings of Rumi; In Search of the Lost Heart: Explorations in Islamic Thought;* and *Imaginal Worlds: Ibn al-Arabi and the Problem of Religious Diversity,* just to mention three from his long list.

Franklin D. Lewis' *Rumi: Past and Present, East and West* (One World, 2000) has also been used. Lewis freshly translated many passages from Movahhed's gathering together in Persian of the Shams fragments, *Maqalat-e Shams-e Tabrizi,* edited by Mohhad-Ali Movahhed (Tehran: Salami, Entesharat-e Khwarwazmi, 1990).

Refik Algan and Camille Adams Helminski have also worked on the Shams material: *Rumi's Sun: The Teachings of Shams Tabriz* (Morning Light Press, 2008). I have not consulted their work to make these versions.

1. #192, p. 284 (622).
2. #156, pp. 265–66 (215).
3. #73, p. 215 (778–79).
4. #11, p. 239 (273).
5. #62, pp. 209–10 (684–85).
6. #91, p. 227 (103–5).
7. #109, p. 238 (710).
8. #71, p. 214 (139).
9. #70, p. 214 (122).
10. #65, p. 211 (779).
11. #134, p. 250 (267).
12. #179, p. 277 (740).
13. #133, p. 249 (744).
14. #112, p. 239 (743).
15. #112, p. 239 (743).
16. #72, p. 214–15 (695–96).
17. #63, p. 210 (751).
18. #70, p. 214 (121–22).
19. #28, #29, #31, p. 192 (681, 767, 224–25).
20. #31, pp. 192–93 (732).
21. #125, p. 246 (629, 303).
22. #127, p. 246 (243–45).
23. #168, pp. 271–72 (243–45).
24. #193, p. 284 (692–93).
25. #191, pp. 283–84 (309).
26. #130, p. 247 (261).
27. #155, p. 265 (641).
28. #193, p. 285 (268–69).
29. #108, pp. 237–38 (105–6).
30. #95, p. 230 (760).
31. #187, p. 281 (219).

32. #188, p. 282 (234–35).

33. #88, p. 224 (646).

34. #221, p. 305 (760).

35. #219, p. 304 (766).

36. #217, p. 303 (168–69).

37. #189, p. 283 (183–84).

38. #206, p. 292 (763–64).

39. #207, pp. 292–93 (98–99).

40. #85, pp. 222–23 (756–57). Also see Gamard and Farhadi, p. 593, note on No. 1898.

41. #85, p. 223 (756–57).

42. #220, p. 305 (1633–64).

43. #34, p. 194 (138–39).

44. #37, p. 195 (610–11).

45. #38, p. 195 (317–18).

46. #143, p. 257 (101–3).

47. #91, p. 228 (103–5).

48. #80, p. 219 (188–89); #81, p. 219 (219–20).

49. #16, p. 45 (202); #17, p. 46 (668); #18 p. 46 (27).

50. p. 36, unreferenced epigraph for section 2.

51. #147, pp. 260–61 (132–33).

52. #202, pp. 288–89 (759).

53. #203, pp. 289–90 (155–56).

54. #204, p. 290 (93).

55. #103, pp. 233–34 (84–85).

56. #181, pp. 278–79 (615–16).

57. Lewis, p. 200. He references Movahhed's Persian text, Maq. #231, #655, #648, #221.

58. Lewis, p. 182. Maq. #163–64.

59. Lewis, p. 136. Maq. #18 and #41.

60. Lewis, p. 148. Maq. #294–95.

61. Lewis, p. 162. Maq. #778–79.

62. Lewis, pp. 162–63. Maq. #777.

63. Lewis, p. 163. Maq. #661.

64. Lewis, p. 163. Maq. #186.

65. Lewis, p. 163. Maq. #119–20.

66. Lewis, p. 164. Maq. #79.

67. Lewis, p. 165. Maq. #749.

68. Lewis, p. 166. Maq. #142.

69. Lewis, p. 200, 202. Maq. #221, #687, #162.

70. Lewis, p. 161. Maq. #622, #290, #618–19.

71. Chittick, section 2, "My Path to God," #12, #8, #9, #10, #11, p. 43, p. 42 (241, 307, 648, 659, 188).

72. Chittick, #205, p. 290 (69–71).

Index of First and Memorable Lines

RUMI

Every day the sun girds up, pulls its
  belt tight, 128
Every day you bring me
  soul-promptings, 52
Every floating bit of dust, 119
Every house without a lamp, my
  friend, 116
Everyone wants union with you, 125

Find your place and close your
  eyes, 22
First, you hold me in your arms, 63
For a long time I stood delighted, 93
. . . Forget memory, 130
For one like you, love is beauty, 107
For the old ones, being small, 101
Friend, could anything be more
  pleasure, 80
From wildflowers in the field, 82

Gamble everything for union, 72
Get up. Turn around the *qutb* of your
  time, 55
Green of the garden, every tree,
  solitude, 62

. . . He, or she, is riding a horse of
  great longing, 54
. . . He brings symbols through me, 104
Here is a subtle truth, 35
Here we are in this clay and water
  mud, 30
How much longer, 68

I am a mirror, as well as someone, 66
I am a mountain. What I say, 37
. . . I am a taste of something *inside*
  you, 73

I am grumpy about one thing, 23
I am not this body, this form, 73
I am not this one you see. If I were
  that *me,* 106
I am so near my friend, 130
I am the guest of music, 127
I am the one who loves your face, 48
I ask the reed flute, Why are you
  crying?, 32
. . . I came in visible form, a cloud,
  128
I come to the beloved in an offhand, 97
I did not know your company in the
  cave, 47
I do not say much, 87
If you become a lover of that face, 126
If you find yourself, even for a
  moment, 74
If you leave this life, I will leave my
  life, 82
If your hands cannot do work, 99
If you were to string together a
  hundred long days, 76
I have a friend who is my sun, 64
I have been around these ecstatic
  lovers, 71
I have been running, 61
I have filled all the paper made in
  Egypt, 131
. . . I have longevity, inside this
  dying, 23
. . . I have no way to go away from
  you, 94
. . . I have one inside my heart who
  creates all color, 87
I have read so many stories, 75
. . . I have thrown a stone and broken
  your water jar, 43

Index of First and Memorable Lines

SHAMS